CULTURE SMART!
ZAMBIA

Andrew Loryman

·K·U·P·E·R·A·R·D·

ISBN 978 1 85733 877 5

British Library Cataloguing in Publication Data
A CIP catalogue entry for this book is available from the
British Library

First published in Great Britain
by Kuperard, an imprint of Bravo Ltd
59 Hutton Grove, London N12 8DS
Tel: +44 (0) 20 8446 2440 Fax: +44 (0) 20 8446 2441
www.culturesmart.co.uk
Inquiries: sales@kuperard.co.uk

Series Editor Geoffrey Chesler
Design Bobby Birchall

Printed in India

About the Author

ANDREW LORYMAN, after graduating with an M.A.Ed. from Brunel University, London, lived and taught in Zambia for twenty years, working in mission, government, private and mine schools in Western, Central, and Lusaka Provinces. Formerly the national coach for the Zambia men's volleyball team, and for many years chairman of the schools' volleyball association, he has spent time in every province in the country. During his years in Zambia he also wrote articles for the *Zambia Daily Mail*, using the name Sitali Mulenga, and with his wife, who is Zambian, ran a chain of hair salons and a tailoring business, and kept 2,000 chickens and ducks on a small farm.

contents

Map of Zambia	7
Introduction	8
Key Facts	10
Chapter 1: LAND AND PEOPLE	**12**
• Geography	12
• Climate	17
• The People	18
• A Brief History	24
• Present-Day Politics	37
• Government and the Judiciary	39
• The Economy	42
• Zambia in Africa	48
Chapter 2: VALUES AND ATTITUDES	**50**
• The Zambian Character	50
• Family and Other Relationships	51
• Gender Roles	54
• Religion and Sorcery	56
• Attitudes Toward Homosexuality	59
• Attitudes Toward Time	60
• Work and the Informal and Formal Sectors	60
• Wealth and Status	62
• Attitudes Toward Foreigners	63
Chapter 3: CUSTOMS AND TRADITIONS	**64**
• Public Holidays	64
• Traditional Storytelling and Proverbs	65
• Traditional Tribal Ceremonies	67
• Coming of Age Ceremonies	70
• Traditional Medicine	71
• Baptism	73
• Funerals	74

• "Sexual Cleansing"	77
• Marriage	78

Chapter 4: MAKING FRIENDS | **84**
• Socializing	85
• Forms of Address	86
• Greetings	88
• The Opposite Sex	89
• Mixed-Race Relationships	90
• Lending Money	91
• Conversation	91
• Invitations	92

Chapter 5: THE ZAMBIANS AT HOME | **94**
• A Roof Over Your Head	94
• Daily Life	97
• Food and Drink	99
• Payday and More	105
• Putting On the Style	106
• Education	109

Chapter 6: TIME OUT | **112**
• Eating Out	112
• Nightlife	114
• Sports	115
• Music and Dance	118
• Art and Crafts	121
• Places to Visit and Things to Do	122

Chapter 7: TRAVEL, HEALTH, AND SAFETY | **124**
• Arrival	124
• Getting Around the Country	127
• Around Town	129

contents

- Roads and Driving 130
- Where to Stay 133
- Health 137
- Safety 139

Chapter 8: BUSINESS BRIEFING 140
- The Business Environment 140
- Business Culture 143
- The Role of NGOs 145
- Personnel 145
- Meetings 148
- Presentations 149
- Business Diplomacy 150
- Contracts and Legal Considerations 150
- Tenders 151
- A Level Playing Field 151
- Gift Giving 152
- Corruption 153

Chapter 9: COMMUNICATING 156
- Language 156
- Body Language 158
- Humor 158
- The Media 159
- Telephone and Internet 161
- Mail 163
- Conclusion 163

Further Reading 165
Index 166
Acknowledgments 168

Map of Zambia

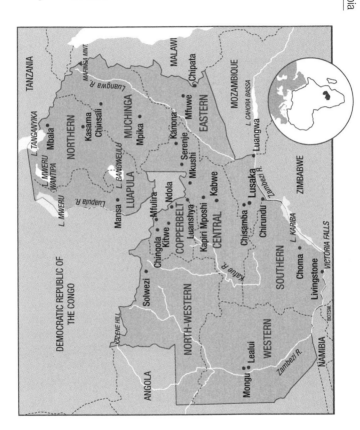

introduction

Zambia is big! It is larger than the combined size of Germany and Norway. Lake Bangweulu and its wetlands alone cover an area larger than Northern Ireland, while the Kafue National Park is bigger than Wales. This landlocked country in central southern Africa is named after the mighty Zambezi River, which rises in the remote Kalene Hills in its northwest. Mineral-rich, with huge untapped agricultural, water, energy, and human potential, it sits on the investor's leader board for Africa.

Zambia has a stunning landscape of forest, woodland, and grassland, traversed by mighty rivers whose journeys are marked by floodplains, swamps, waterfalls, lakes, and long, languid loops to the sea. David Livingstone, the Victoria Falls, Lake Kariba—these magical names, together with the spectacular wealth of bird and wildlife and the range of luxurious lodges and tented camps set in the African countryside, make it the upscale safari destination of choice. The city of Livingstone is the high-octane capital of southern Africa, offering bungee jumping, zip-lining, river rafting, and other activities for those seeking an adrenaline rush.

Apart from the obvious tourist attractions, Zambia is also a living celebration of multiculturalism. It is a potpourri of traditions, ceremonies, and customs taken from seventy-two ethnic groups, and as English is widely used it is easy for foreigners to engage with its lively, good-humored people.

The Zambians have moved through diverse tribal histories, European colonization, socialist philosophy and rhetoric, and, finally, a gung-ho charge into multiparty capitalism in the early 1990s. Today Zambia is a forward-thinking democracy, with life played out against the backdrop of unspoiled countryside and rich cultural traditions. It is one of the most urbanized countries in sub-Saharan Africa—more than 40 percent of the population live in urban areas. The burgeoning tourist industry, the presence of huge mining organizations, and the growth of commercial farming enterprises have all had an impact on Zambian society, sharpening the distinction between traditional village life, largely unchanged for centuries, and modern urban life, whether in exclusive gated communities, rented apartment blocks, or unplanned shanty towns.

By and large the Zambians are taking this change in their stride. Their equanimity and geniality are based upon a carefree attitude to life and the realization that worrying about something doesn't actually ameliorate the problem: it's better, as the Chewa say, to smile and show your teeth—"*Kukondwa ndi kuonetsa mano!*"

Culture Smart! Zambia goes beyond the tourist panorama of pristine nature and the busy urban life, luxury hotels, shopping malls, and rush-hour bottlenecks of the big cities. It describes the psyche of a people who have been shaped by their geography and history, who are notable for their warmth, outgoing nature, and zest for life. We hope to offer an insight into the feelings, behavior, and ideas that permeate Zambian society, to enable you to understand your hosts more fully and so make the most of your stay.

Key Facts

Official Name	Republic of Zambia	Independent on October 24, 1964
Capital City	Lusaka	Pop: 2.179 million
Main Towns and Cities	Kitwe, Ndola, Kabwe, Chingola, Mufulira, Livingstone	10 provinces, each with a provincial capital
Area	290,587 sq. miles (752,618 sq.km)	
Topography	A high plateau drained by the Congo River in the north and the Zambezi and Kafue Rivers in the south, west, and center, with low areas in and around the river valleys. Five major rivers, 4 major lakes, and more than 20 waterfalls, including the Victoria Falls	
Population	17,403,875 (2017)	Growth rate: 2.94% (est.)
Age Composition	0–14: 46.08%; 15–24: 20%; 25–54: 28.65%; 55–64: 2.91%; 65+:2.35% (2016 est.). Median Age: 16.7	
Ethnic Makeup	The main tribes are the Bemba, the Tonga, the Chewa, the Lozi, the Nsenga, the Tumbuka, and the Ngoni.	There are 72 tribes. Main non-African minorities: Chinese, Indian, European
Climate	Generally dry and temperate, tropical; modified by altitude	The Zambezi and Luangwa Valleys are particularly hot just before the rains.
Seasons	Three seasons: warm and wet Dec.–Apr.; cool and dry May–Aug.; hot and dry Sept.–Nov. Highest rainfall in Mbala in north, 64 ins. (1633 mm); lowest rainfall in Livingstone in south, 39 ins. (981mm).	
Resources	Copper, cobalt, coal, emeralds, gold, water, wildlife, timber	Africa's second-largest copper producer after the DR Congo

Life Expectancy	Male 50.8, female 54.1	Infant mortality: 62.9 deaths/1000 live births
Languages	Official language: English. Main local languages: Bemba, Lozi, Lunda, Luvale, Nyanja, and Tonga	70 other indigenous languages and dialects spoken throughout Zambia
Literacy Rate	70.6%	
Religion	Christianity is the largest faith. Minority groups are Muslims and Hindus.	In 1996, the Constitution recognized Zambia as a Christian nation.
Government	Multiparty democratic republic. The National Assemblly, directed by the speaker, is a unicameral parliament consisting of 150 elected members and up to 8 members nominated by the president.	
Media	Zambia National Broadcasting Corporation has 2 TV channels and 4 radio stations.	19 TV channels, incl. subscription. 88 radio stations. 24 Internet news media outlets (2016)
Currency	Zambian Kwacha (ZMW)	1 USD = 10.23 ZMW (2017)
GDP Per Capita	US $1,269.6 (2016)	GDP growth 3.2% (2015)
Electricity	220–240 volts, 50 Hz	Square 3-pronged plugs used. US appliances need adapters.
TV	PAL B/G system	
Internet Domain	.zm	
Telephone	Zambia's country code is 260.	Area codes: Lusaka 0211, Kitwe 0212, Livingstone 0213
Time Zone	GMT+ 2 hours	

chapter one

LAND &
PEOPLE

GEOGRAPHY

Zambia was known as "The Real Africa," or so the old
Zambia National Tourist Board proclaimed—a slogan
that purveys the notion of an Africa of old where
time stands still and Karen Blixen and the big-game
hunter Denys Finch Hatton continue to play out their
smoldering *Out of Africa* relationship in a colonial
setting. The real Africa today has more to do with the
relatively unspoiled landscape and its diversity.

An eclectic mix of high plateau and low-lying
valleys, Zambia is spectacularly endowed with wildlife,
having more than a hundred species of mammals and
more than seven hundred species of birds. To these
resources can be added the formidable Victoria Falls,
where the Zambezi River plunges more than 350 feet
(108 m); the vast Lake Bangweulu; Lake Mweru; the
southern tip of Lake Tanganyika; and Lake Kariba. In
the west of country is the Zambezi floodplain, which
in April, after the end of the rainy season in March,
resembles a huge inland sea.

Stretching across the interior heart of the plateau
of southern Africa, Zambia lies between latitudes 8°
and 18°S, and longitudes 22° and 34°E. The Central
African Plateau slopes gently southward toward
Mozambique, but in the northeast of Zambia the land

rises toward the Mafinga Mountains, climbing to more than 7,644 feet (2330 m) on the border with Malawi.

The plateau is dominated by the passage of three huge rivers—the mighty Zambezi and its tributaries, the Kafue and the Luangwa. Created by the formation of rift valleys three hundred million years ago, these three rivers drain the plateau and provide for the extraordinary features that make up the country. They contribute hugely to Zambia's biodiversity and complex ecosystems, and are of vital economic importance.

The Zambezi rises in the Kalene Hills in the North-Western Province, near the border with the Democratic Republic of the Congo (DRC), before flowing southwest through Angola and reentering Zambia, where it assumes a width of more than 1,300 feet (400 m). It is Africa's fourth-longest river, and flows for 1,677 miles (2,700 km) into the Indian Ocean at its mouth on the Mozambique coast, its basin covering an area greater than the Republic of South Africa. Eight countries in the region—Zambia, Angola, Namibia, Botswana,

Zimbabwe, Malawi, Tanzania, and Mozambique—are directly linked into this vast river system.

The Zambezi flows southward. Deep gorges cut into the basalt rock cause the river to form stunning whitewater rapids, creating the small Chavuma Falls and the more spectacular, horseshoe-shaped Ngonye Falls, near Sioma, in the Western Province. Now the river flows eastward at an altitude of nearly 3,000 feet (more than 900 m) into the Caprivi Swamps, where it is joined by the Chobe River. Here, Zambia, Botswana, Namibia, and Zimbabwe meet. The swamplands end in the swirling white waters of the Katambora Rapids. The river then flows smoothly on until it hurls itself over the precipice that is the Victoria Falls. Named by the local Bakololo in the 1800s as Mosi-oa-tunya, meaning "the smoke that thunders," the Victoria Falls is a UNESCO World Heritage site and a premier tourist attraction in Zambia and neighboring Zimbabwe.

Passing through a series of gorges with rapids and smaller falls, the Zambezi is subsumed by the man-made Lake Kariba, more than 124 miles (200 km) from the Victoria Falls. Lake Kariba is the largest

reservoir of fresh water in the world, with six floodgates. The dam wall was completed between 1955 and 1959. The Zambezi continues to flow eastward before being joined by its tributary, the Kafue River, near Chirundu. Bisecting the Lower Zambezi National Park in Zambia and the Mana Pools National Park in Zimbabwe, the Zambezi is joined by the Luangwa River at the town of Luangwa. Still flowing eastward, it has once again been dammed, to create the Lago de Cahora Bassa in Mozambique.

While better known for its magnificent whitewater landscapes, the Zambezi also creates the huge Barotse Floodplain in the Western Province, where, at the end of the rainy season, the river can reach a width of about sixteen miles (25 km). This annual flooding directs the lives of the Lozi people who live there and provides the very rich soil that overlies the coarse, infertile Kalahari sands of this region.

A Garden on the Sand

For newly arrived staff at the girls' mission school in Mongu, Western Province, a trailer-load of rich, black, alluvial soil taken straight from the Barotse Floodplain was an important settling-in gift. Spread generously, like a chocolate topping, over the coarse-grained Kalahari sands and retained within a primitive stick fence, it could comfortably provide a household with fresh vegetables for the duration of a contract. This gift from the Zambezi would eventually disappear as time went on, merging with the sand and forgotten.

The Kafue River is the longest river wholly within Zambia, rising just south of the border with the DRC.

Its basin covering an area of more than 60,600 square miles (157,000 sq. km), the river flows south and then east from the Copperbelt, passing through the Kafue, Lochinvar, and Blue Lagoon National Parks. The Lukanga, Busanga, and the Kafue Flats are wetlands of international significance. Dams have been built across the river at the Itezhi-Tezhi gap and at the Kafue Gorge for the production of hydroelectricity.

The second tributary of the Zambezi, the Luangwa, occupies the western section of the Great Rift Valley, with Lake Malawi occupying the eastern part. The river flows for about 500 miles (800 km)

southwestward, with the Muchinga Escarpment on its western side. With its floodplain, oxbow lakes, and pronounced meanders with sand banks, the Luangwa Valley has a rich diversity of carnivores and herbivores and an important safari business, with thirty or more facilities catering to tourists.

For something out of the ordinary, the Great Bangweulu Basin, which includes the vast Lake Bangweulu and its wetlands, is located in a depression in the northeast of the Zambian Plateau, near the border with the DRC. Seventeen rivers feed the basin from a catchment area of more than 73,000 square miles (190,000 sq. km), but only the Luapula River drains it. This beautiful, undisturbed corner of Zambia is home to the extraordinary-looking shoebill stork, and is the only place in the world where the black lechwe antelope are found.

CLIMATE

With the country at an average height of more than 4,000 feet (1,200 m), the climate is greatly moderated by altitude, and it is only in the Zambezi and Luangwa Valleys, where the land falls to below 1,640 feet (500 m), that high temperatures occur in September and October. Here the humidity is high during the wet, or rainy, season. For the most part the climate is tropical or subtropical, with three distinctive seasons: cool and dry from April to August, hot and dry from August to November, and warm and wet for the remainder. Lusaka, the capital, has an average June temperature of 50.2°F (10.1°C), an average October temperature of 88.3°F (31.6°C), and a mean annual rainfall of 31 inches (800 mm).

The rainfall decreases broadly from north to south, with Mbala at 5,488 feet (1,633 m), near the border with Tanzania, receiving a mean annual rainfall of 45 inches (1,140 mm), and Livingstone at 3,236 feet (981 m) a mean annual rainfall of 29 inches (740 mm).

As the temperature increases when the year moves toward November and the humidity rises, heavy downpours can be expected around lunchtime or early afternoon. Torrential rain can cause havoc on the roads, and potholes and landslides are inevitable consequences. Enterprising youngsters eagerly fill the craters with rocks and soil—and extend a hand for payment.

Rain on a Hot Tin Roof

Corrugated thin-gauge steel, actually. When the rainy season arrives, schools, offices, and industries inevitably have to go on "Talk Loudly" mode, assuming that any communication is to be maintained. As a teacher, the options are to raise your voice and shout information against a backdrop of deafening drumming or simply to abandon the lesson and invite students to gaze joylessly out of the windows as another drenching is assured when they leave the classroom.

THE PEOPLE

There are ten provinces in Zambia, each with districts; in order of population, largest first, they are: Lusaka, Copperbelt, Eastern, Southern, Central, Northern, Luapula, Western, North-Western, and Muchinga. Each province has a minister and a permanent secretary who is the administrative head, each appointed by the president. Unsurprisingly, Lusaka Province has the highest growth rate, and Muchinga Province the lowest. Overall, the population of Zambia shows a growth rate of 2.88 percent (2014), but with the urban population expanding at an average rate of nearly 4 percent (2015), some 45.7 percent of the population are expected to live in urban centers by 2025. Outside Lusaka, most of the large towns are found in the Copperbelt, with

Kitwe, Ndola, Mufulira, and Luanshya the biggest. This growth reflects the importance of the copper industry and related secondary industries that supply the mines. Outside the Copperbelt, the "line of rail" settlements stretch from Kitwe to Livingstone, and have experienced growth together with the provincial administrative centers known previously as British Overseas Management Administration (BOMAs). Zambia, in common with many African countries, has experienced a massive movement of people, mainly hoping to secure work, from the countryside to the cities. Larger towns and cities have seen the inexorable growth of informal settlements, or shantytowns, with more than 70 percent of the urban population living in such settings. Indeed, in the ten years following independence, when population growth was about 13 percent per year, it was hardly surprising that formal housing could not keep pace.

Under the slogan "One Zambia One Nation," Kenneth Kaunda's United National Independence Party sought to provide a rallying cry for the seventy-two tribes (ethnic groups) that made up the country and, with English as the lingua franca, linguistic and tribal differences were to be set aside. Today the large towns and cities are a confusion of cultures, with a migrant population from all corners of the country but, significantly, homogeneous in terms of the language spoken. Within the forty-five informal settlements in Lusaka, it is imperative for a newcomer to speak Chinyanja, while in the Copperbelt most of the inhabitants of the ninety-five informal settlements speak Chibemba.

The traditional tribal boundaries of Zambia have been used to forge the country's ten provinces and administrative areas.

The Bemba

Twenty-one percent of all Zambians are from the Bemba
tribe, most living in the Northern, Luapula, Muchinga,
and Copperbelt Provinces. Tracing their origins to the
Luba–Lunda Empire of the southeastern part of the
DRC, the Bemba people have an important centralized
chieftainship led by Paramount Chief Chitimukulu.
Traditionally, the Bemba live in villages, with each family
cultivating cassava and millet in a small area outside the
village. They may also grow beans, maize, sorghum, and
sweet potatoes. The poor quality of the soil means that
the fertility is quickly lost, and shifting cultivation—
known locally as *chitemene* cultivation—is practiced, in
which trees and scrub are cut and piled up before the
ritual lighting of this biomass to create a thick layer of
ash. This is dug into the ground to improve the soil; but
ultimately the result is deforestation, and the ground has
to remain fallow for many years. Today, with reduced
basal dressing costs, and with the assistance of the
Farmer Input Support Program, this destructive practice
is less evident, and the sweeping fires along the roads in
Northern and Luapula provinces during the dry period
are less frequent.

The Ngoni, Chewa, Nsenga, and Tumbuka

By the mid-nineteenth century, in the Eastern
Province, the warlike Ngoni (4 percent of the
population), related to the Zulu of South Africa,
had conquered the Chewa (7.4 percent), the Nsenga
(5.3 percent), and the Tumbuka (4.4 percent), who
had all originated from the Luba–Lunda Empire. Since
then, the Ngoni language has been entirely replaced
by Nyanja (Chichewa) in the province and many
Ngoni customs have disappeared, though the Nc'wala
ceremony, held in February to celebrate the first

harvests, is one of the cultural highlights of a nation that honors its heritage. (See Chapter 3, page 67.)

The Tonga

The Tonga people (13.6 percent), who live in the southern part of the country, are traditionally pastoralists, with herds of sheep and goats. They are said to love their animals, and supposedly your first greeting to a Tonga person should be an enquiry after his cattle! There is a distinctive Tonga breed of cattle that is ideally suited to the plateau and valley areas of the south. With a small frame and widespread medium-sized horns, this predominantly brown breed is used for meat, though slaughter is usually likely to take place only for a wedding or a funeral—this reflects the increasing importance of bride wealth, and these cattle are referred to as *ngombe lya mukowa* (cattle offerings). Herds can be seen roaming the miombo woodland adjacent to the Lusaka to Livingstone road, and this region has the highest distribution of cattle, goats, and sheep in Zambia. The miombo woodlands cover a large area of northern Zambia; the vegetation is grassland and shrubs, dominated by miombo trees.

The Lozi

The other great cattle herders are the Lozi (5.7 percent) of the Western Province, whose lives center on the Zambezi River and its great floodplain. With a distinctive royal family, the Bulozi Kingdom was established in around 1550 and the *litunga*—the king, or paramount chief (*litunga* is a Luyana word, meaning "nation")—effectively holds all the land on behalf of his people, including some twenty-five other tribal groups. Working with the *indunas* (stewards and councilors), the *ngambela* (prime minister) guides the *litunga* over local issues and court proceedings in a highly structured society. Of interest is the sight of sledges, pulled by oxen, skimming across the sand carrying farm produce, materials, and people.

The Lala, Lenje, Kaonde, and Lunda

With so many ethnic groups or tribes, it is impossible, within the confines of this book, to provide even a brief introduction to each, but it would be useful to highlight the larger groupings in the provinces not yet covered.

In the Central Province, the Lala (3.1 percent) peak a dialect of Bemba, live mainly in Serenje District, and rely heavily on subsistence farming, growing maize, sweet potatoes, beans, cassava, and millet. Near Kanona, north of Serenje, are the magnificent Kundalila Falls.

The Ila and Lenje, also from the Central Province, are part of the Bantu Botatwe (Three People) group and, along with the Tonga, make up 15 percent of the population. Like the Tonga and Lozi, the Ila people value their cattle as a source of status and wealth, with money earned from paid employment being invested in cattle.

The Kaonde (2.9 percent) live in the North-Western Province and in the Kaoma District of Western Province. The history of copper mining in Zambia began with the Kaonde digging for copper at Kansanshi six miles (10 km) north of Solwezi, the provincial capital of North-Western province, back in the fifth century, where the copper was traded as jewelry in the form of crosses and bangles. Today, two enormous open-pit mines owned by Kansanshi Mining PLC make this largest copper mine in Africa.

The Lunda (2.6 percent), of which there are very many subgroups, are the most populous people in the North-Western Province, with many found in Angola and the DRC as well. The Lunda are forever associated with the Fisher family, who have lived in the area since 1905, when the British surgeon Walter Fisher set up an early medical mission. Today the Kalene Mission Hospital and Nursing School and orphanage serve a population of some 44,000 people.

Minority Communities

The Asian community (the term that is used to refer to Indians, both Muslim and Hindu), the white community, and the Chinese community are comparatively small in numbers, but have added greatly to the country's development and culture. The Asians were traditionally traders with small shops who were able to obtain and sell a vast array of products even in the 1970s and '80s, during the Kaunda era, when imports and foreign currency were severely restricted. Highly successful, with enterprises in every province except the Western Province, where the *litunga* forbade their settlement, this community has long been important in the manufacturing sector.

The white community has made a significant contribution to the tourist industry over the last thirty years, and many of the companies that organize adventure and leisure vacations, safaris, and tours are owned and managed by them. In addition, there has always been a small white farming community, with particular concentrations in Chisamba, Ngwerere, and Mkushi. With an influx of commercial farmers from Zimbabwe and South Africa, many of them entering with an Investor's License, this number is expected to grow.

With Chinese investment estimated at US \$5.6 billion, and with some 280 business enterprises in the country, the Chinese community has grown considerably from the days of the workers' camps sited along the TANZAM (Tanzania–Zambia Railway) opened in 1975. Today, China is the third-largest investor in the country, with both state and private participation.

A BRIEF HISTORY
Prehistory

Human habitation in Zambia goes back some two million years. In 2001 Professor Larry Barham discovered, on a ridge overlooking a lagoon in the Luangwa Valley, some Oldowan stone tools that indicate early Stone Age settlement. They are similar to tools found in the Olduvai Gorge in Tanzania, and also resemble choppers and hand axes found near the Victoria Falls.

More sophisticated Early and Middle Stone Age tools of the Acheulean tradition, with distinctively shaped hand axes and digging sticks produced by *Homo erectus*, have been found near the Kalambo Falls in the north. Here, evidence of the use of fire with hearths, charred logs, and charcoal indicates a

growing practicality in dealing with the cold and with formidable predators. Around the same time, the three Mumbwa Caves, west of Lusaka, show that early humans were using fire and had constructed simple windbreaks to shield the mouths of their caves.

In 1921 the first early human fossil found in Africa was discovered in Broken Hill (now Kabwe). The skull of Broken Hill Man, together with other bone fragments, has been dated to 200,000 to 300,000 years old. They were thought to be related to an early ancestor of *Homo sapiens* found in Africa, named *Homo heidelbergensis* because of an earlier discovery of similar remains near Heidelberg, in Germany.

Some 15,000 years ago, the Late Stone Age period began in Zambia, characterized by specialized equipment for hunting and fishing, such as bows, arrows, and hooks. Kafue Iron Age sites at Itezhi-Tezhi show evidence of formal graves and more tools.

At this time, rock art found in caves and shelters— particularly in the Eastern Province, in the Lukusuzi National Park, and in the Northern Province, where the Mwela Rock Art Site is a UNESCO World Heritage Site—teaches us much about the history and culture of prehistoric communities. The Mwela Rock Art Site has more than a thousand paintings.

Ancient Zambia

Evidence shows that the Stone Age inhabitants of Zambia closely resembled the San people of the Kalahari in Botswana, who relied on hunting and the gathering of fruits, roots, and tubers. These people were eventually superseded by or integrated into the populations of Bantu-speaking peoples (there are about five hundred Bantu languages, recognized by shared linguistic features) from west and central Africa. These people followed at least three routes of migration—from the great lakes, from the Congo Forest, and from Angola. Gradually the population of this part of Africa began to change, with sites being selected for settlement and cultivation as people brought with them the ability to make iron agricultural implements to clear the land; it was seen that their iron-tipped weapons were more efficient than those used by the early settlers. The reason for the migration of the Bantu-speaking people is not known, but it may reflect the growth of population in their own lands, with the consequence that resources could not support them, or climate changes.

The more settled lifestyle saw the domestication of goats and sheep and the building of "pole and dagga" (sticks and mud) huts arranged in small groups. These villages began to flourish, and the seventh century saw the smelting and, importantly, the trading of copper. The significant trading post of Ingombe Ilede ("the place where cows sleep," in the local language) established by the Tonga people on the left bank of the Lusitu River (a tributary of

the Zambezi) grew up at this time, being strategically situated for copper from the north and gold from the south. Here, rich grave goods of gold ornaments, copper crosses, and glass beads indicate a prosperous society trading with the gold fields in Zimbabwe and using the Zambezi

as an important trade route. As trade continued, a governing class developed, a plutocracy assuming control and producing a ministate.

Ethnic Groups
Between the sixteenth and nineteenth centuries, groups of people, clans, with a similar language and a common cultural background, tended to join together and develop an identity that transcended family or clan. This larger group, the tribe, could successfully dominate a region, and it is during this period that the Bemba and Lunda in the north, the Lozi in the west,

and the Chewa in the east attained significant power. Their ascent was due to the growth of the powerful Lunda Empire centered upon Katanga Province in what is now the Democratic Republic of the Congo. These groups have a paramount, or senior, chief.

In the southern part of Zambia, prior to the arrival of the British colonialists, the Tonga people were divided into matrilineal clans in small, scattered villages. The colonial officials found it expedient to appoint prominent Tonga tribesmen to become village chiefs, thereby facilitating government policy. A rank order of chiefs exists today and the Tonga are the second-largest ethnic group after the Bemba.

Settlers from the South—"*Mfecane* Victims"

From 1817 to 1850 southern Africa was devastated by wars and the wholesale dislocation of populations. Referred to as the *Mfecane* (from the isiZulu word meaning "the crushing"), this turmoil had dramatic consequences for the area that was to become Zambia. The causes were complex, and reflect a range of factors. The expansion outward from the Cape Colony by European settlers inevitably caused conflict, and the rise of the militaristic Zulu kingdom under Shaka kaSenzangakhona (the Zulus were a subclan of the Nguni, originally a part of the great Bantu migration) and their defeat of rival Nguni nations created deep instability, as the vanquished tribes fled northward.

A rebel Zulu general, Mzilikazi, defeated by Shaka in 1817, welded his own Ndebele people with local tribes and went on to wreak havoc in the Transvaal. Upon defeat by the incoming Dutch Voortrekkers, he crossed the Limpopo River in 1838 and entered the western part of modern Zimbabwe. Here the Ndebele encountered the Makololo people, who had themselves been driven out of their kingdom in what is now Lesotho by Shaka. Fleeing north, the Kololo defeated the Luyuna on the Zambezi Floodplains and, under Sebitwane, established their own rule (interestingly, shortly before he died, in 1851, Sebitwane met with David Livingstone, the Scottish missionary working for the London Missionary Society). In 1864 the Luyana, by this time known as the Rotse or Lozi, regained their land, and today they speak a mixture of Luyana and Kololo known as Silozi.

In eastern Zambia, further trauma occurred with the arrival of marauding Ngoni warriors under Zwangendaba, who sought cattle and slaves for the Portuguese traders who had moved inland from the Mozambican coast. Driven north after conflict with Shaka's *impis* (regiments), these raiders crossed the Zambezi in 1835 and proceeded to pillage and destroy the local Chewa and Tumbuka villages up to the border with modern-day Tanzania. One group settled near Chipata, under the chieftainship of Mpezani.

By the turn of the nineteenth century, this region of Africa was a patchwork of different ethnic groupings, each with its own culture and oral traditions. The advent of European explorers and traders was to change all that.

Contact with Europeans

The Portuguese, who had already established settlements in Guinea and Angola on the west coast, began to take great interest in the gold wealth associated with the ruler Munhumutapa in present-day Zimbabwe. They established a trading station in 1531 at Tete, some 260 miles (418 km) upstream from the mouth of the Zambezi on the Indian Ocean. With a toehold in this part of Africa, and with a thriving slave trade to Brazil emanating from their territories on the Atlantic, it is not surprising that the Portuguese made incursions into the interior. Interestingly, the Portuguese word *sapato*, meaning shoe, is identical to the Bemba word for a shoe. Later the Chikunda (former Portuguese slaves), the Bemba, and other northern tribes joined the Arab–Swahili slavers to fill the markets in Zanzibar and the Mozambican ports. The Scottish missionary and explorer David Livingstone had firsthand experience of the slave trade in this region, and was greatly saddened that African tribes had resorted to selling slaves to the Portuguese traders.

ENCOUNTERS WITH SLAVERY—DAVID LIVINGSTONE

"No one can understand the effect of the unutterable meanness of the slave-system on the minds of those who, but for the strange obliquity which prevents them from feeling the degradation of not being gentlemen enough to pay for services rendered, would be equal in virtue to ourselves. Fraud becomes as natural to them as 'paying one's way' is to the rest of mankind."

David Livingstone, *Missionary Travels and Researches in South Africa*. London: John Murray, 1857

"To-day we came upon a man dead from starvation . . . One of our men wandered and found a number of slaves with slave-sticks on, abandoned by their master from want of food; they were too weak to be able to speak or say where they had come from; some were quite young."

Horace Waller, ed., *David Livingstone, The Last Journals of David Livingstone, in Central Africa, from 1865 to his death*. London: John Murray, 1874.

Arriving in South Africa in 1841, David Livingstone spent more than thirty years as a missionary and explorer, and during his three great expeditions came to realize that the way to defeat the slave trade was by the legitimate trading of commercial goods. In a famous lecture delivered in 1856 to a packed audience in the Senate House of Cambridge University he declared triumphantly,

"I beg to direct your attention to Africa. I know that in a few years I shall be cut off in that country which is now open. Do not let it be shut again! I go back to Africa to try to make a path for commerce and Christianity. Do carry on the work which I have begun. I leave it with you!" For Livingstone, it was imperative that the industrial might of Victorian Britain be harnessed for the good of the African people, and that improved social and economic conditions be implemented to destroy the slave trade and ensure that the local population became more inclined to convert to Christianity.

On May 1, 1873, David Livingstone died at Chief Chitambo's village in an area south of Lake Bangweulu. Desperately ill with dysentery and hemorrhaging severely, he died while attempting to find the source of the Nile. Famously, his two followers, Chuma and Sousa, interred his heart and organs under an *mpundu* tree in the village and carried his embalmed body back to Zanzibar.

A funeral followed in Westminster Abbey, with Livingstone's four children present, as well as H. M. Stanley, who had met Livingstone three years earlier at Ujiji, near Lake Tanganyika. Today the David Livingstone Memorial twenty-one miles (35 km) north of the Kasanka National Park marks the spot where his heart and organs were buried.

Perhaps Livingstone's greatest legacy was the arrival, shortly after his burial, of missionaries from Europe. Indeed, his death precipitated an almost unseemly haste to bring in the gospel, medical care, and schools, with various evangelical Churches establishing mission stations. François Coillard from the Paris Evangelical Missionary Society established mission stations across Barotseland (western Zambia), and Henri Dupont of the Catholic White Fathers (Missionaries of Africa) did the same in northern Zambia.

The British South African Company (BSAC) was chartered in London in 1889 by Queen Victoria. The imperialist industrialist Cecil Rhodes, having invaded Mashonaland and benefiting from duplicitous dealings with Lobengula, the son of Mzilikazi, had created a huge trading area for the BSAC, which was to become Southern Rhodesia, now Zimbabwe. Turning his attention to the area north of the Zambezi, the Company was able, deceitfully, to get the king of the Lozi people, Lewanika, with François Coillard at his side, to sign over all mining and trading rights to the BSAC.

The Lochner Concession effectively handed control of Barotseland to the Company in 1890.

After punitive action against Mwata Kazembe X of the Luba–Lunda people in the north and Mpezani of the Ngoni, the BSA Company was effectively in control. The new territory was referred to as Northern Rhodesia (BSAC's Northwestern Rhodesia was joined with BSAC's Northeastern Rhodesia), with Livingstone as the new capital, in 1911. Cecil Rhodes' vision of a Cape-to-Cairo railway was nearer fruition, and railway sidings, halts, mining camps, administrative camps, and market places became new urban centers in this embryonic nation.

Colonial Rule

In 1923 the BSAC charter was revoked and Southern Rhodesia became a self-governing colony of Britain. Northern Rhodesia became a British protectorate in April 1924. The new protectorate was seen to have few resources and consequently the BSAC was able to keep the mineral rights, together with large tracts of land.

The early years of this new protectorate saw the migration of men to work in the gold fields of South Africa. Prompted by the need to pay the newly instituted "Hut Tax," men from Barotseland and the south migrated in large numbers in a recruitment drive organized by the Witwatersrand Native Labour Association, known as WENELA, and by the mines in Katanga (in the Democratic Republic of the Congo), popular with men from the Luapula area. Ironically, this preceded a move of labor to the north of the country in the mid- to late 1930s, as the huge copper ore deposits of the Upper Kafue Basin, in what became known as the Copperbelt, were exploited.

Problematically, despite the revenue generated by the two big companies in Northern Rhodesia, Rhodesian Anglo-American, and the Rhodesian Select Trust, taxes were paid to the British government in London and royalties to the BSAC, which still owned the mineral rights. Little money was therefore available for local Northern Rhodesian development, and with increasing taxes and poor conditions in the mines, strikes and riots occurred in late May 1935—the year that Lusaka became the capital.

The Growth of Nationalism

Against a backdrop of growing disturbances in the copper mining areas of Northern Rhodesia in 1940, organized by the Northern Rhodesian Mine Workers Union, it became clear that there was an increasing desire for self-determination and government among the African workers. In 1948, the first political party for Africans grew out of the Federation of Welfare Societies as the Northern Rhodesia Congress, with Godwin Lewanika from Barotseland as its first president. In 1951, the party changed its name to the Northern Rhodesia African National Congress, with Harry Nkumbula as its president, and in 1953 Kenneth Kaunda became the general secretary.

With growing African aspirations and African representation in the legislative councils of Nyasaland (Malawi) and Northern Rhodesia, and all-African Town Management Boards in the copper mining areas, the European minority in Northern Rhodesia felt uneasy. In addition, the economy in Southern Rhodesia, with its larger white population, was in a bad way, and the economic significance of profits being taken from the north to boost its coffers was seen as a way to maintain white settler domination.

In October 1953, despite protests from African leaders, the Federation of Rhodesia and Nyasaland was created. With large grants from federal funds

going to the development of the south, politicians in Northern Rhodesia and Nyasaland became increasingly skeptical about the union, with living standards hardly improving and African people denied the same rights as the European settlers. Roy Welensky, a former railway worker from Broken Hill (Kabwe), became the Federal Prime Minister in 1956, and with the slow rate of progress toward a more egalitarian society, the black middle class throughout the Federation began to campaign for greater fairness in what had been designated as a partnership between ethnic groups.

In 1959, as a consequence of the increasing civil disobedience and rioting, a state of emergency was declared. Nationalist political parties such as the Zambia African National Congress (ZANC) under the leadership of Kenneth Kaunda, were banned. The bringing in of white Southern Rhodesian troops to curb the agitation in the Copperbelt deeply disturbed the Colonial Office in London, and the Monckton Commission, preparing for the

1960 Federal Review Conference, reported the deep animosity felt by black Africans. Northern Rhodesia and Nyasaland, it said, should be allowed to leave the Federation.

Independence

By the end of 1963 the Federation was terminated and a new constitution for Northern Rhodesia was drawn up. The elections of January 1964 were convincingly won by the United National Independence Party (UNIP), formerly the ZANC, and the new government entered into negotiations with Britain regarding independence.

On Saturday, October 24, the Queen's representative, Princess Mary, welcomed the newest member of the Commonwealth and handed Kenneth Kaunda the Instruments of Independence. At this time the new Zambia had fewer than a hundred university graduates, two doctors, and fewer than a thousand African secondary-school graduates. Heavily dependent upon  fluctuating copper prices, trade routes through the southern ports and through Portuguese colonies, and reliant upon Rhodesia for 60 percent of all her imports, this young country was facing great difficulties. The Republic of Zambia became a member of the United Nations on December 1, 1964.

The Kaunda Era

Kenneth Kaunda—known affectionately as KK—and the United National Independence Party (UNIP) established a government that would rule the country for twenty-seven years (1964–91). He dominated the political scene, introducing a social philosophy, wide-ranging economic reforms, and a trend for safari suits! He also habitually carried an iconic white handkerchief, which he waved about like a traditional flywhisk. Kaunda and his ministers established a humanism-based, state-controlled economy, which oversaw the emergence of huge parastatals controlling

the running of the mining, transportation, financial, commercial, and manufacturing sectors. The one-party state operated as a one-party participatory democracy, with the electorate free to choose their UNIP Members of Parliament from a selected party shortlist, and with Kaunda as the sole presidential candidate.

By the early 1980s, with falling copper prices and rampant fiscal and managerial mismanagement, Kaunda was forced to accept International Monetary Fund and World Bank support that would open the economy to a free-market-based structural reform program with maize subsidies removed and public expenditure reduced. By 1987 the economy had deteriorated to such an extent that Kaunda suspended contact with the global moneylending agencies and reestablished price controls on basic commodities and the use of local resources to reduce the dependence on imported goods—the end of Coca-Cola and Fanta, and the emergence of Kwench and the excitingly named Jolly Juice! Such were the shortcomings of this New Economic Recovery Program (NERP)—which marked the end of the economic liberalization and left the country with high inflation, increasing debt, and falling production and prices—that the UNIP government was forced to go back to the IMF and the World Bank in 1989, when a new package was drawn up entailing the removal of subsidies and price controls, the devaluation of the currency, and the retrenchment of thousands of civil servants and parastatal workers.

In June 1990 an army officer took over the state radio station for several hours, announcing a coup. For Kaunda and UNIP the writing was on the wall as opposition groups formed the Movement for Multiparty Democracy (MMD) in the following month, after rioting in Lusaka as a consequence of huge food price hikes. In December of the same year Kaunda signed a constitutional amendment marking the end of twenty-seven years of one-party rule and opening the way for the first multiparty parliamentary and presidential elections in October 1991, which saw the MMD sweep into power with landslide victories.

PRESENT-DAY POLITICS

Zambia can be justifiably proud of its achievements in terms of multiparty politics. Gone are the dark days of the one-party state (interestingly, Zambia had a multiparty system at independence) and its tenets of humanism and communocracy. Gone too, are the vastly inefficient ZIMCO (Zambia Industrial and Mining Corporation) parastatals, and forgotten, too, are the facts that many shops were taken over by the state from Asian traders, who were accused of hoarding, and that Zambia was bordering on being a police state.

Since the 1991 elections Zambia has had six presidents, the incumbent being the lawyer Edgar Lungu of the Patriotic Front (PF). The return to multiparty politics in 1991 has seen the rise of many political parties—at the 2016 elections there were forty-six registered parties but only nine were able to pay the registration fee by the deadline date. The August 2016 elections saw the president reelected in a closely contested vote, with the result rejected by the main opposition party, the United Party for National Development (UPND). The Electoral Commission said that Edgar Lungu had received 50.35 percent of the votes, while his closest challenger, Hakainde Hichilema of the UPND, received 47.63 percent. This election marked the first time that the winner needed more than 50 percent of the vote to avoid a runoff, with the delays in finalizing the results prompting the opposition's allegations of malpractices and irregularities.

President Lungu, who had previously served as minister of justice and defense in the previous PF government under Michael Sata, has his support base in the Eastern Province, Lusaka, and the Copperbelt, and among the Bemba-speaking regions. A Christian, President Lungu has established a Ministry of National Guidance and Religious Affairs and overseen the introduction of a National Day of Prayer.

The opposition leader, Hakainde Hichilema, is a wealthy businessman, ranch owner, and economist, popular with young, middle-class voters. With his support base in the Southern, Western, and North-Western Provinces, he narrowly lost by 27,757 votes in the January 2015 presidential elections, called after the death in office of President Michael Sata in October 2014. A footnote to the death of Michael Sata was that Guy Scott, the Vice-President, became the first white Zambian leader since independence.

Since the introduction of multiparty politics, Zambia has had an enviable record in terms of the peaceful transfer of power. However, the violence and the inflammatory language used by politicians and the media in the runup to the 2016 elections show the fractured nature of its politics, with a countrywide split between the two main political parties. The results revealed a clear division between the UPND-supporting south and west and the PF-supporting north and east. Clearly there is still a need for recourse to the "One Zambia, One Nation" refrain, but it is worth remembering that Zambia was only the second country in Africa to remove an incumbent president in 1991, and that the nation was able to repeat that feat in the 2011 elections.

GOVERNMENT AND THE JUDICIARY

The elections in 2016 saw voting on a new constitution to enhance the Bill of Rights contained in Part 111 of the Constitution, the election of local government officials, and the election of MPs and the president. The president is elected for a five-year term and as well as being the head of state and government he is also the commander-in-chief of the defense force. The National Assembly (Parliament) has 156 members directly elected on the basis of a simple majority under the first-past-the post system and not more than eight nominated members. It also consists of the vice-president (running mate), the speaker, and the first and second deputy speakers.

The laws of Zambia consist of (a) the Constitution; (b) the laws enacted by Parliament; (c) statutory instruments; (d) Zambian customary law, which is consistent with the Constitution; and (e) the laws and statutes that apply or extend to Zambia, as voted for. The judicial system is based upon English common law and customary law. The Supreme Court is the highest court in the land and serves as the final court of appeal, while the High Courts administer common law and have the power to hear civil and criminal cases. The Subordinate Courts, presided over by Resident Magistrates' Courts, are found in all the districts and can try any offense under the written laws of Zambia. Cases relating to marriage, inheritance, and property under African Customary laws are referred to local courts.

Zambia has 287 chiefs, administered by the Ministry of Chiefs and Traditional Affairs, and the House of Chiefs is a department within it. The House serves as an advisory body to the government on traditional and customary matters, and the chiefs, with the support of their councilors, are able to settle disputes within their territories. The issue of customary or traditional land (held and administered by the chiefs on behalf of the people) is an important matter for the traditional rulers, and since this land does not officially have title the chiefs and headmen have an important role in ensuring that the people benefit.

Sitting in Judgment

Chief Mwansakombe Chifumbe Chintlelwe of the Ngumbo people of Luapula Province is my brother-in-law. Situated on the Samfya to Kasaba road, his "Palace" provides shelter, storage, and, importantly, a place for hearing local squabbles, disagreements, and accusations. Outside, there is a timetable written in ink on a pink card:

> MONDAY, WEDNESDAY, AND THURSDAY
> SPECIAL CASES ONLY
> 08.00 hrs to 13.00 hrs
> 13.00 hrs to 14.00 hrs – Lunch
> 14.00 hrs to 17.00 hrs
>
> TUESDAY and FRIDAY
> 08.00 hrs to 09.00 hrs – Reports, Summons, Complaints
> 09.00 hrs to 13.00 hrs – Court Session
> 13.00 hrs to 14.00 hrs – Lunch
> 14.00 hrs to 16.00 hrs – Knock Off
>
> SATURDAY
> 08.00 hrs to 13.00 hrs – Only Very Special Cases
>
> PLEASE OBSERVE TIME
> BY ORDER

Inside, the tables are piled high with folders spilling papers, bookcases filled with books and more folders, and the chief sits composed behind his narrow, formica-topped desk, pen poised. Around him are anxious faces, people sitting on white and green plastic chairs, headmen, and a *kapaso* (a government employee who acts as a general assistant) resplendent in a khaki uniform and with a GRZ (government) cap badge. There are tales of chicken theft, missing cassava plants, lost goats, and accusations of witchcraft.

THE ECONOMY

The Gross Domestic Product for Zambia reached US $1,269.6 per capita in 2016, showing a growth rate of 3.22 percent. Mining remains the mainstay of the economy and the discovery of huge deposits of copper ore in the North-Western Province has enabled the industry once again to support the nation.

Zambia is a young country. Almost half the population is below the age of fifteen, and with a high fertility rate (the joint-second-highest in Africa), Zambian women on average have 6.2 children. It has been projected that the population will increase by 811 percent to more than 140,348,000 by 2100—among the highest growth rates in the world. It is not surprising, therefore, that the child dependency ratio creates enormous pressure on the productive population in the country.

The vast number of children and young people orphaned as a consequence of AIDS puts an extra burden upon those in employment and who have their own family responsibilities. The extended family is truly extended, often to the breaking point, without any safety nets. The visitor to Zambia will not fail to notice, in among the vibrancy, color, and sights, the countless children who inhabit the streets, the city outskirts, and the villages in rural Zambia—ragged, barefoot, but bright-eyed and smiling.

A high population growth (3.2 percent annual change) obviously feeds into the high unemployment rate of 13.3 percent and the growing number of young people without jobs. Some 4 million are without work, and these represent a source of concern as entrenched poverty and subsequent instability sets in, particularly in the urban areas. Today responsible middle-class Zambian families limit the number of children that they have as they take into account their financial needs. Educated women in the wealthiest fifth of the population are likely to have fewer than four children, whereas poorer women without education have more than eight.

Copper Mining, Minerals, and Gemstones

Today, copper exports account for 73.8 percent of Zambia's total exports, and copper remains the largest foreign exchange earner; but, as always, there are questions of world price volatility and what happens when the copper runs out.

Copper extraction has taken place in Zambia for over a thousand years, with practically the entire production centered upon the Copperbelt. The story goes that in 1902 a prospector, William Collier, shot a roan antelope that fell on copper-stained rocks in a clearing on the banks of the Luanshya stream—with the absence of vegetation further indicating the presence of copper.

Initially poor-quality oxides on the surface were exploited, but it became clear that by drilling deep underground a vast new resource could be tapped. With the Second World War looming, expansion proceeded apace with copper components needed for weapons. New mines were opened and existing ones were refurbished or expanded. In 1969 the Copperbelt produced 750,000 metric tons.

Production has risen from 251,000 metric tons in 2002 to 710,000 in 2015, largely due to the opening up of three mines in the North-Western Province with the latest, Kalumbila, starting operations in 2014. These multimillion-dollar operations have changed the provincial capital, Solwezi, and indeed the lives of the Kaonde people of this region with a vast array of new infrastructure put in place by the mining companies.

Globally, Zambia is the world's seventh-largest copper producer and the second-largest in Africa, though the industry has not been without its problems. Fluctuating copper prices reflect an economic downturn in China, and production in Zambia has been affected by "load shedding." This occurs when a utility company does not have enough energy to meet the demands of its customers and therefore needs to resort to interrupting the supply.

The copper mining companies consume vast quantities of electricity for their operations, and although the government has largely protected them, at the expense of ordinary citizens, production has been affected. The situation became so bad that in 2015 the government imported power from Mozambique to ease the deficit—ironically from the Cahora Bassa HEP project on the Zambezi River downstream from the Kariba power station.

Recently a new 300-megawatt coal-fired power station constructed by Maamba Collieries Ltd. in the Southern Province has come on stream. Critics point to the high carbon emission from such a plant at a time of global warming and the push for clean energy. More appropriate, perhaps, and a better long-term investment, is the construction of solar plants similar to the two plants of 50 MW each in the Lusaka South Multi-Facility Economic Zone.

Zambia has just embarked on a rather more extreme way to end load shedding by engaging the Russian state nuclear agency Rosatom to build a nuclear plant within the next ten to fifteen years. The same Russian company built a reactor in Iran. This facility is expected to produce two gigawatts of electricity, the same as the current amount produced in South Africa. Of course, concerns have been raised about the availability of water to cool the reactors (the low levels at Lake Kariba have exacerbated the load shedding), the lack of technicians, and what happens to the spent nuclear fuel—and why not properly harness the enormous water resources and the opportunities for solar energy?

Cobalt (a by-product of copper mining), gold, uranium, and a variety of gemstones are all extracted, with the deep-green emeralds being particularly valued. Zambia now produces 20 percent of the world's emeralds from the Kagem open-pit mine in the Copperbelt.

Agriculture

With nearly 300,000 square miles (nearly 78 million sq. km.) of land, 40 percent of which is suitable for arable farming, and a climate that lends itself to year-round cultivation, the potential is huge. Since independence it has been obvious that there needs to be a move away from the fluctuating fortunes of copper toward a more diversified economy, with agriculture at the forefront. This has not been helped by the large South African food chains, which import fruit and vegetables from South Africa.

The majority of Zambian farmers are small-scale farmers dependent on hand tools for cultivation, and rain-fed maize remains the principal crop. Sowing takes place in October/November, and harvesting in May/June. As always, the challenge has been to enhance the sector's capacity to achieve mass-production and to feed into the agro-manufacturing subsectors, and here subsidized fertilizer costs and the premium rates (30 percent higher) offered by the Food Reserve Agency for maize have seen production rise by 10 percent to 2.87 million tonnes for the 2015/16 season with exports to Malawi.

As well as maize, the small-scale farmer may also grow cassava, millet, sorghum, sweet potatoes, and

groundnuts (peanuts), and invariably keeps "village chickens"—scrawny scavengers that move through yards and gardens looking for food.

Maize is also produced by commercial farmers, but their principal row crops have been soybeans and wheat, which may be irrigated or rain-watered. Commercial farmers have also overseen a huge increase in livestock farming, including beef and dairy cattle, poultry, and pig production.

Fishing

Remarkably, bearing in mind that Zambia has some of the best water resources in Africa and holds 40 percent of the water resources in the SADC, the country imports an estimated 40,000 metric tons of fish every year with bream (tilapia) from China available in most supermarkets. Accounting for a paltry 1 percent of GDP, yet with more than 300,000 people involved in the industry and of crucial importance to the rural economy, fishing has been sadly undervalued.

The need to grow and sustain this sector in Zambia is beginning to be met with the promotion of aquaculture parks and the advancement of the industry in high-potential areas of the Northern, Western, and Southern Provinces. With the simultaneous development of processing technology and fish feed, together with the growth of fish farms, it is expected that this largely untapped resource will contribute much more to the economy in the future.

Manufacturing

With an average annual growth rate of 3 percent and accounting for 11 percent of the country's GDP, manufacturing is centered upon agro-processing (food and beverages) and the leather and textiles subsectors. The manufacturing of metal products, fertilizers, explosives, chemicals, and cement is significant in Lusaka, the Copperbelt, and North-Western Province, where Multi-Facility Economic Zones have been established with appropriate physical and administrative infrastructure in place.

ZAMBIA IN AFRICA

In the 1960s and '70s, Zambia's position as a landlocked country surrounded by hostile white minority governments to the south, east, and west—including Portuguese-ruled Mozambique and Angola, the apartheid state of South Africa, South-African-controlled South-West Africa (Namibia), and Rhodesia—put the country under enormous strain. One of the "Frontline States" during this period, Zambia sought to provide refuge to freedom fighters engaged in liberation struggles. The South West African People's Organization (SWAPO), The National Union for the Total Independence of Angola (UNITA), the Zimbabwe African People's Union (ZAPU), the Zimbabwe African National Union (ZANU), and the African National Congress (ANC) all had offices, camps, and bases within the country at some stage. Indeed, The African Liberation Centre was situated in the Lusaka suburb of Kamwala.

Today Zambia has an enviable reputation for political stability and the post-election transfer of power. The country has been elected to the fifteen-member African Union Peace and Security Council for a three-year term, ending in 2019. It is a member of the Common Market for East and Central Africa (COMESA) and hosts the secretariat, the Southern African Development Community (SADC), and the African Cotton and Textile Industry Federation (ACTIF).

chapter two

VALUES &
ATTITUDES

THE ZAMBIAN CHARACTER

Zambians are a naturally gregarious people,
whose lives are generally unhurried and peaceful.
They are proud of the stability within their
country, which contrasts markedly with some
of the neighboring states. People tend to be
nonconfrontational: they try to find an amicable
solution to a problem rather than cause an upset
that might spoil a relationship. In this respect,
it is often hard for a Zambian person to say
no, preferring instead to vacillate and appear
indecisive. Being blunt and frank is regarded as
being rude and unseemly, and as saying more
about the person who is speaking than the
recipient.

Zambians are unlikely to display anger or
sadness in public, and strongly dislike displays
of impatience. For the visitor, this has particular
implications when encountering the police, or
immigration or customs controls, when a relaxed
and respectful discourse will provide a better
solution. In fact, a display of any kind, apart from
the all-embracing hysteria of sporting success, the
joyful reunion of long-lost female friends, and

laughter at a joke, is generally frowned upon. This is particularly true in the case of a demonstration of affection between a man and a woman. In fact, it is more usual to see male friends and female friends holding hands after the initial handshake in a show of brotherly/sisterly comradeship. Someone may continue to hold your hand long after the initial handshake as a well-meaning gesture of fraternity.

FAMILY AND OTHER RELATIONSHIPS

As in many African countries, there is a great gulf between rural and urban, traditional and modern. The growth of urban dwelling and wage earning has drastically altered village life, with the young no longer feeling the need to support their kin who have stayed behind. Now it's more a case of everyone for him or herself, and to make ends meet as best they can.

In a traditional society based upon a subsistence economy, the growing of crops, the keeping of animals, together with fishing and hunting, were communal activities where large families were seen as an asset. In order to maximize output, the more people who were able to contribute, the better. This society was better able to absorb the old, infirm, widowed, and orphaned, and better able to provide communally for school fees, *lobola* (bride price), weddings, and funerals. This was the extended family, where people were brothers and sisters rather than cousins, mom and dad rather than aunt and uncle. It provided communal wellbeing instead of individual pauperism for the villagers.

Family Values

My wife's uncle was Chief Mwansakombe Xth Chifumbe IVth. A large, corpulent gentleman, he was of the old school, a traditional chief, with five wives and forty-six children, though it was rumored that he had fifty-three.

He is buried at Kumushitu, near Chikwanda, a village on the edge of Lake Bangweulu in Luapula Province. It is the customary burial place for chiefs, and is ordinarily accessed only when a chief is buried. I was fortunate to be able to visit the site, though under Ngumbo observance my wife, as his niece, was not.

We walked down a dusty, leaf-strewn path, just wide enough for a car, with planted eucalyptus trees on either side. I was escorted by a gentleman I can only describe as the "keeper of the gate," who carried a bowl of white powder (probably maize flour), and four other villagers. Our journey to the graves was marked by a short halt for a ritual incantation, while kneeling, to show respect to the spirits of the chiefs, and the throwing of some of the powder to appease the spirits of the ancestors laid to rest there.

As we neared the graves, we knelt again, and more white powder was sprinkled as the keeper lifted a branch that had been placed across the path. Eight graves were situated at the base of a row of ancient, gnarled trees. Hippo teeth had been placed on some of the grave mounds, and each grave was identifiable to the keeper. The place was hauntingly beautiful, and here my brother-in-law, the present chief, will one day be laid to rest.

The town and city dweller in Zambia today may suffer the demands of the extended family with less grace than before, and may regard those in need less kindly. Modern people are more concerned about their own immediate family and their requirements in an "every man for himself and let the devil take the hindmost" society. The nuclear or elementary family seeks to distance itself from kith and kin, with members seldom making a visit to their rural heartland and almost despising their relatives who journey to town to seek help. Modern Zambia hasn't quite descended into putting elderly relatives into care homes yet, but they can be sent back to the village and cared for by their close and extended family members. Perhaps the saddest indictment of modern Zambian society is seen when those working abroad in well-paid jobs fail to keep in touch with their parents back home, adopting an "out of sight, out of mind" mentality as they inch forward in life's race.

Of course, anyone living abroad is assumed to be wealthy. Zambians abroad are likely to be besieged with requests for help with school or university fees and medical costs, and, should they ever step foot in the old country again, they are sure to be inundated with relatives eager to share in their good fortune.

The notion of the extended family is somewhat complicated by the presence of members who may be of "same father, different mother," or "same mother, different father" relationships. All are welcome, and are regarded as brothers and sisters regardless of when they arrived into the family.

GENDER ROLES

In traditional Zambian society a woman's place was in the home, having children, looking after them, working in the fields, and tending the livestock. The village woman never stopped working, and it is still the same today. From the rising of the sun to its setting, a woman's work is an unending series of tasks—fetching water from a well that may be some distance away, tending children, washing clothes and dishes, preparing and cooking food, and the small matters of digging, sowing seeds, weeding, and finally harvesting alongside the men. Then there is the firewood to collect from the forests—huge bundles of branches lashed together with long strips of bark twine and carried back to the village on the head. It's backbreaking work, and often accomplished while holding one child by the hand and carrying another in a cloth slung on the back.

It is assumed that in all things women should defer to men. For years a woman has been virtually little more than a useful appendage, good for sustaining a home and a family, and ensuring that her husband's every need is attended to. The husband is the bread-winner, and therefore more deserving and more useful.

From a young age, girls in the village are regarded as domestic helpers and given such responsibilities as cooking, cleaning, and caring for the young, the old, and the sick. Their opportunities to pursue an education are further limited by the fact that Zambia has one of the highest rates of child marriages in the world. Under traditional law, marriage can take place at puberty; 8.5 percent of girls are married by the age of fifteen, and 41 percent by eighteen.

The Zambian government is actively looking to find ways of bringing young girls back into education after they have been taken out of school to be married. The term used is "rescued from marriage," and chiefs and NGOs have been urged to assist in this. Of course, the

problem for the state is that giving a girl in marriage brings in *lobola*, the bride price of negotiated cash or kind that her family receives from the bridegroom. Although in Zambia the Marriage Act has established a legal age for marriage (eighteen for women and twenty-one for men), and the Penal Code makes sex with a girl below the age of sixteen an offense, these controls rarely apply under customary law.

Today the modern city-dwelling young woman seeks to be independent, and to make her own way without having to be deferential and submissive. She is educated, motivated, and in no hurry to settle down with a husband and children: Western rather than traditional, carefree rather than tied. The modern upper-class family, moreover, will have workers—cleaners, drivers, gardeners—to ease its way through life.

RELIGION AND SORCERY

On December 29, 1991, the newly elected, born-again president of Zambia, Frederick Chiluba,

declared Zambia as a Christian nation, and in 1996 this was enshrined in the constitution. The constitution provides for freedom of religion, and there is no discrimination based on religious belief or practice. Of interest is the fact that members of parliament are not allowed to quote from the Bible in Parliament.

The construction of the 10,000-seater National House of Prayer in Lusaka, with an advisory board appointed by the president, is testimony to the government's commitment to Christianity. With more than 95 percent of the population confirmed Christians, the influence of the early Christian missionaries is plain to see, with most being Roman Catholics, Anglicans, Baptists, Methodists, Seventh-Day Adventists, or Jehovah's Witnesses. The spread of Kingdom Halls, belonging to the Witnesses, along all the major roads reflects the large number of congregations in the country—more than 2,800.

There are small Muslim and Hindu populations in the larger towns, and some distinctive areas of settlement, with mosques and temples. The Kamwala and Luburma/Madras district of Lusaka has a large Muslim residential and retail area.

The Pentecostal movement is perhaps the fastest-growing Church in Zambia, and is particularly popular with young people. Loud, vibrant, and with an emphasis on a miracle-working God, it seen as the antithesis to the staid established Churches. The new Churches are not without controversy, however, as shown in the Northern Province, where a pastor was admonished by the Evangelical Church of Zambia for selling anointed pants, brooms, oil, and water!

Religion is very important to the average Zambian, and attendance at church is regarded as a time for both worship and fellowship. Best clothes are worn, as members seek to use the spiritual world to influence their physical being, both materially and emotionally. Prosperity preaching in the style of American televangelists is vociferous and animated, and altar calls for healing are positively received. It has been suggested that the enormous growth of the Pentecostal Churches may be a response to the AIDS pandemic of the 1980s.

Like most people from Africa, Zambians are deeply spiritual, and, of course, the traditional African belief system predates later religious influences. While most groups have a belief in a creator, or Supreme Being, there is also an underworld inhabited by spirits that can determine life, death, disease, wellbeing, and even the weather. The Supreme Being is known as Lesa in Bemba, Nyambe in Lozi, Mulungu in Nyanja, and Leza in Tonga, and the spirits might be individual or ancestral. An individual spirit or entity can cause changes in character or violent, uncontrollable behavior (there is a link here with the biblical casting out of demons and the deliverance/cleansing associated with Pentecostal Churches). An ancestral spirit contributes to good fortune and success; without proper appeasement, it may bring bad luck.

The fact that Zambia has a Witchcraft Act says much about the prevalence of witches and witch-finders in the country. Belief in witchcraft is widespread, and success, failure, good health, or illness can be attributed to it. A witch or wizard can be hired to improve one's business or to shatter lives and, through incantations, sacrifices, and a variety of rituals, can invoke spirits to act on their behalf.

In places where superstitions exist, rumors can turn deadly. Perhaps crops have failed, someone has died, or a well has dried up. What, or who, has caused these mishaps? Someone needs to be blamed. In many districts in Zambia, individuals or vigilante groups have murdered people suspected of practicing witchcraft, and witch-finders have been deployed. Among the Kaonde of North-Western Province, the practice of *chikondo* (pointing finger), also known as "flying coffins," is used to find the identity of a murderer. The coffin containing the body of the victim is lifted up by family members who have taken hallucinogenic bush medicine. The corpse leads them to whoever committed the crime, the guilty are soundly beaten, and compensation is demanded. Not surprisingly, the guilty are invariably wealthy. An interesting *modus operandi* was used by a witch-finder in Kazangula District, who found three witches suspected of killing a boy by using a radio-cassette player and a leaf. An assortment of charms was found in the suspects' houses.

Perhaps the most celebrated use of charms and witchcraft was discovered when a former finance minister and one-time foreign minister was discovered to have used witchcraft paraphernalia to evade capture for three months. The police apparently resorted to the services of a witch-finder to capture him, and reported that when he was found he was wearing charms and had a fetish that allowed him to be invisible.

There is an excellent witchcraft exhibition at the Lusaka National Museum, where you can see the fetish that allowed the wearer to steal crops from a neighbor's field, and a snakeskin belt that helped a sorcerer sleep with another man's wife while her husband was in the same bed!

ATTITUDES TOWARD HOMOSEXUALITY

With some 98 percent of the population (2010 survey) disapproving of homosexual behavior, it is not surprising that same-sex sexual activity is illegal in Zambia. The penal code bans sodomy, which is punishable by fourteen years to life in prison.

Zambia is one of thirty-six African countries that outlaw same-sex sexual behavior, and this deeply devout Christian nation is torn between accepting a God who loves all humanity and the anti-gay rhetoric of Church ministers who see Africa as one of the last bastions against the depravity of a malignant, spreading gay lobby. Today Zambians are asking whether they can worship a homophobic God, and whether the religious zealots who occupy the pulpits really know what God wants.

For some Zambians, however, the issue has more to do with the temporal than the spiritual, with human rights to the forefront and the removal of any law that discriminates on the basis of sexual orientation. If heterosexuality is a sexual orientation permissible under law, then why not homosexuality, they argue.

Either way, Zambia has a community of homosexuals whose private lives are closeted and for whom a heterosexual marriage may be necessary to mask their orientation. Lusaka and the Copperbelt, with their many straight bars, restaurants, and clubs, absorb many whose lifestyles are at odds with the law.

ATTITUDES TOWARD TIME

Zambians have a relaxed attitude toward time, with most organized events and social appointments having a flexible element that can allow for margins of a couple of hours. Punctuality may be stretched and elongated, which accounts for the need to wait in line for buses and in banks, and for the general tedium of bureaucracy that delays everyone.

Zambians will acknowledge their shortcomings in this regard, and will jokingly bow to the respected punctuality of Europeans, offering a multitude of plausible explanations for their tardiness. The bottom line is, of course, that in a country as informal and relaxed as this, time doesn't really matter, and social occasions are never marred by such transgressions.

Zambians are masters of the twenty-four-hour clock, and "a.m." and "p.m." are never used. Visitors must get used to 07:00 hours, 14:00 hours, 22:00 hours, and so on, and not confuse 16:00 hours with 6:00 p.m.!

WORK AND THE INFORMAL AND FORMAL SECTORS

Everyone has to work, and in a country with no social services safety net, and where school fees must be paid for children over fourteen, it is not surprising that any work is regarded as better than none. Educating a child may be nominally free to the end of Grade 7, but each school requires a "user fee" to be paid, and then there are school uniforms and exercise books to be purchased. Piecework, or short-term work, is very common, and groups of dayworkers wait on street corners in town for an early morning pick-up.

With 90 percent of workers in the informal sector, the country is full of entrepreneurs who can turn their hand to anything, or are eager to try. How many homes and businesses with substandard building, plumbing, or electrical work bear testimony to the exuberant but unqualified skills of laborers who are cheap? Go to a market, and you'll see the informal sector hard at work, with men and women selling, making, and repairing—no taxes paid, and a nominal fee for a peddler's and hawker's license.

Street vending is regarded as a necessary evil, as it is a source of employment for large numbers of unemployed and underprivileged town and city dwellers who lack finances and skills. The government over the years has had a love–hate relationship with vendors and has built new modern markets to accommodate them, but the vendors keep returning to the streets. Recently, a Street Vendors Empowerment Scheme established in the Copperbelt, Lusaka, and Central Provinces has seen 2,500 youths benefit from low-interest loans. Many streets in the urban centers are lined with young and old selling vegetables, fruit, buns, clothes, and cooking oil—mini-supermarkets with smiling assistants and cashiers. Try them, and the Zambian custom of asking for an *mbasela* (a little extra to thank you for your patronage).

It's not just the urban streets that have strings of businesses. Take the road out of Lusaka and discover the tomato mountains near Banani International School, the watermelon mounds near Liteta, and the "Irish" potatoes near Chimupati on the Great North Road. There are tabletops of peanuts, sweet potatoes, plastic containers of honey, and fertilizer bags of charcoal strapped up with bark twine.

You can enter the traffic trying to get into Cairo Road during the rush hour and purchase a charger and "talk-time" for your cell phone, haggle over a jacket, try on a pair of polyester trousers with comfort waist, or a shirt, *bwana*? Buy a rabbit, a puppy, or the latest Jean-Paul Gaultier see-through midi-dress in flimsy chiffon for Madam?

Private company employees in the formal sector on pay-as you-earn, whose tax is deducted at source, contributing directly to the government's coffers, are comparatively few in number. Most work in the mining and quarrying industries, construction, the wholesale and retail trades, finance and insurance, and the agricultural sector. The largest employer is the government, and a job here is guaranteed for life, though the pay and allowances are poor.

Zambia has three state universities and nineteen private universities (as of 2016) offering a huge range of courses and producing most of the country's white-collar workers. This thriving country is expanding rapidly, and a look at any Zambian online employment page will reveal a plethora of opportunities all in urban areas, especially Lusaka. Of course, with so many graduates, competition is fierce.

WEALTH AND STATUS

Money doesn't equate to value, of course, and people should never be valued by their income or net worth, but it helps if you want to book a table in a good restaurant. In Zambia the cult of the celebrity and big money does exist, with acolytes hovering around musicians, singers, and soccer players. Big cars and fast cars are a draw, and extravagance is seen as a necessity when it comes to mingling with the masses, especially if you are young.

Politicians and ex-politicians do fairly well, with lots of handshakes, bowing, and fawning. It is a fact of life that comparatively few appear accountable for their shortcomings and misdemeanors, and even the condemned approach VIP status when in public.

ATTITUDES TOWARD FOREIGNERS

Most Zambians are very friendly, and visitors from abroad find this to be a bonus. They are curious, and eager to learn and to hear your opinions about their country and life in general. You can get used to being called *Mukuwa* (Lozi/Tonga) or *Muzungu* (Nyanja/Bemba)—meaning "white person"—and being trailed by bands of barefoot, beaming ragamuffins as you walk through villages or any of the shanty towns. Staccato cries of "How are you?" and "Can I have sweet?" ring out, reflecting the rote learning of English in the primary schools. Being polite, and responding with, "I am fine, and how are you?" always works very well, and will draw out more huge smiles.

One interesting fact is that a Zambian will call an Afro-American or someone with a Caribbean background *Muzungu* principally because that person doesn't speak a Zambian language or understand anything of the culture. It would appear that race is only one part of being a *Muzungu*.

Zambians usually find Europeans and North Americans easier to socialize with as a result of English-language familiarity and cultural similarities. The sense of humor and general repartee between the groups makes for a lot of fun on an evening out.

While Zambians mix readily with anyone, there is usually more formality with people from the Indian subcontinent (*Mwenye*) and China, where cultural and social norms are different. There are, of course, language barriers for many of the Chinese.

chapter three

CUSTOMS & TRADITIONS

PUBLIC HOLIDAYS

Zambia has fourteen public holidays since the addition in 2015 of the National Day of Prayer and Fasting, when bars, pubs, and restaurants are closed. For most districts, parades and processions are the order of the day, and very entertaining they are. Lots of suits,

PUBLIC HOLIDAYS	
January 1	New Year's Day
March 8	Women's Day
March 12	Youth Day
Good Friday	
Holy Saturday	
Easter Monday	
May 1	Labor Day
May 25	Africa Freedom Day
First Monday in July	Heroes' Day
Day after Heroes' Day	Unity Day
First Monday in August	Farmers' Day
October 18	National Day of Prayer, Fasting and Reconciliation
October 24	Independence Day
December 25	Christmas Day

special uniforms, caps, hats, banners, and, of course, hair—permed, black or bleached, box-braided— stride past various dignitaries who stand on a platform. The bands play martial music and the synchronized office and factory workers, college students, and school children swing arms with beaming teachers, turning stern heads toward the platform.

The holidays are an excellent opportunity to take in some of Zambia's cultural offerings, and a celebration wouldn't be the same without drumming and dancing. Each school and village has a dance troupe that will take a turn at the local stadium.

TRADITIONAL STORYTELLING AND PROVERBS

Imagine a world without cell phones, tablets, TVs, or radios. A star-strewn, moonlit night, with shadows dancing from a flickering fire—and silence. A storyteller holds court, seated at the center of a group, eyes darting to each person, and voice sonorous, modulating for effect. The village scene is set.

Zambians have always loved sharing traditional stories. African storytelling is very much a communal and participatory event, and an integral part of a child's education. The oral tradition provided continuity in the transmission of culture, history, and behavior, so that successive generations could follow the ethics and values of their people.

Stories and fables allow ideals and morals to be imparted—think of the "Ant and the Grasshopper," or the "Tortoise and the Hare"—and in Zambia the principal characters in many of the stories are Kalulu the Hare, a wise, heroic character; the Elephant and the Hippo, basically comedians, and the Hyena, a scoundrel. These folk tales describe the triumph of wisdom or good over evil, or teach us to consider our thoughts and actions.

It's probably true to say that everyone knows a proverb or two—little one-liners that offer pearls of wisdom and wit. In the village, they may be used to explain events and circumstances, or to shape behavior, and are passed down from generation to generation, instructing and guiding people.

Proverbs from Zambia

Zambian proverbs offer advice on everything for everyone. Look at these literal translations:

If you are ugly, know how to dance.
Tomorrow brings many things.
Start early, before the floods come.
One who enters the forest does not listen to the breaking of twigs in the bush.
To be always looking for an alteration is to look for trouble.
Mother, carry me; I, too, will carry you.
Milk is obtained from a cow that has a calf.
Those who eat water monitors [lizards] are found close to each other.

Despite the many political, economic, and social changes, these small pearls of insight can still be found in the hubbub of twenty-first-century Zambia. On a fun note, check out the "Get Rich Quick or Die Trying" shopping complex on Lusaka's Mungwi Road, or see the modern axioms displayed on minibus windscreens—"God Loves You," "Jesus Saves."

TRADITIONAL TRIBAL CEREMONIES

There are more than fifty traditional ceremonies in Zambia, some small and many large, that take place every year. Jamborees of dance, song, and music spread across the length and breadth of the country, informing and reminding the people of their heritage. One cannot do justice here to such a wealth of cultural traditions, but it is worth mentioning some of the bigger events.

In the "Nc'wala" ceremony, held in February in Chipata, Eastern Province, Paramount Chief Mpezeni of the Ngoni and his chiefs and headmen, resplendent in lion and leopard skins, give thanks for the rains and the abundant harvest. Knobkerries and

cow hide shields are raised, and the ground is stamped in dance, reflecting their Zulu ancestry.

The Lozis of the Western Province periodically celebrate their Kuomboka ("Getting out of the Water") ceremony, around March, for rather more pragmatic reasons: when the Zambezi bursts its banks and the villages on the floodplain are inundated, the *litunga* (paramount chief) and his court move from Lealui on the plain to Limulunga, on higher ground. The Kuomboka is not an annual event, as the water level fluctuates year by year. The most recent Kuomboka was in 2017; the previous one was in 2012.

Majestic in a copy of the British admiral's uniform that King Lewanika was given by Edward VII in 1902, the *litunga* leads hundreds of dugout canoes and royal barges in his iconic vessel, the *Nalikwanda*, to make landfall some hours later at Limulunga. Watch the rhythmic coordinated punting, carried out by royal paddlers, listen to the drums and the singing, and watch the shoulder-shrugging Lozi women dancing.

In July, the Lunda people of Kawambwa District, Luapula Province, led by the senior chief, Mwata Kazembe, reenact the exploits of their forefathers as they migrated from Shaba in the Democratic Republic of the Congo. Every time they conquered a people, the warriors celebrated the victory with a great undying ceremony climaxing in a dance, Umutomboko, performed by Mwata Kazembe himself.

The Lykumbi Lyamizi ceremony is held every August in Zambezi District (North-Western Province) and celebrates Luvale art, history, and culture. The famous Makishi dancers wear elaborate masks made from bark and wood decorated with paper and paint, and pants and shirts made of dyed root fibers. There are more than a hundred Makishi characters representing the spirits of their ancestors, and the

local Luvale people are well aware of which to approach and which to avoid. Each Likishi (singular of Makishi) has a distinctive personality, and everyone knows how each will act when they enter the festival grounds in a masquerade led by King Kayipu, the lead Likishi, named after a famous chief.

There has been renewed interest in Zambian traditional ceremonies since the mid-1980s, brought about as a result of an increasing awareness among city and town dwellers that their particular tribal systems are being slowly eroded by Western culture. Many of the ceremonies are now crowd-funded and supported by wealthy businesses.

COMING OF AGE CEREMONIES

The rite of passage from childhood to adulthood is marked in virtually every tribe in Zambia by initiation ceremonies, with the practice being particularly common for girls.

For boys, the ceremony usually consists of circumcision, and is mainly found in the North-Western and Western Provinces among the Luvale, Chokwe, Luchazi, and Mbunda peoples. The Tonga people hold a short preparation for boys (Gobelo) to explain the rights and duties of marriage, but without circumcision.

The Makishi masquerade mentioned above marks the culmination of a one-month separation of boys from their families as they experience the initiation, or Mukanda. Proclaimed a "Masterpiece of the Oral and Intangible Heritage of Humanity" by UNESCO in November 2005, the Makishi masquerade celebrates the boys' circumcision, the tests of courage that they have undergone, and the lessons they have learned about their roles as men and husbands.

Moreover, in the twenty-first century circumcision is seen very much as part of a long-term HIV strategy to provide Zambian men with up to 60 percent protection against contracting HIV from an infected partner. To date, nearly 73,000 Zambian men have been circumcised under the Centre for Infectious Disease Research in Zambia (CIDRZ) Voluntary Medical Male Circumcision program.

All Zambian ethnic groups have coming-of-age rites for girls, usually at the first menses at the age of twelve or thirteen. Female initiation involves a period of instruction under the supervision of older, usually married, women who specialize in this teaching. The discussing of reproductive matters between parents and their children is regarded as inappropriate in Zambian culture, and it is thought that the task of informing girls on what it is to be a woman, wife, and mother, is better left to others who are practiced in this. The initiation ceremony can last for three days for some groupings—Bemba, Kaonde, Tumbuka, and Chewa—and longer for the Tonga, Lozi, Luvale, and Lunda. There are many differences in the ceremonies, but ultimately, for all ethnic groups, the aim is to provide sex and health education and possibly advice on sexual techniques, with the ultimate aim of pleasing the husband.

The coming out of the girl initiates from the instruction period is regarded as a time of great celebration, and some rural communities make quite a show of their progress into womanhood. In the towns and cities the instruction is likely to be much more private, and some girls are sent back to the villages to receive the teaching.

TRADITIONAL MEDICINE

According to the World Health Organization (2016), at least 70 percent of Zambians use traditional medicine, and there are more than 35,000 members of the Traditional Health Practitioners Association of Zambia, as well as thousands of practitioners who are not members. It's big business indeed, and a part of a Zambian person's heritage, with a tradition of using plants, plant products, and sometimes animal parts carried on for hundreds of years. Of course, before contact with the West, people had already deduced which natural products could heal and cure.

Four's Enough

Mr. Banda, a subsistence farmer from the Eastern Province, has four wives. He married the first, Lizyness, in 1993, but in 1997 he fell in love with Loveness Phiri from a neighboring village and told Lizyness that he wanted to take a second wife. "She was very unhappy, and I understood why, as she wanted to have her husband all to herself," says Mr Banda. In order to placate her, he gave Lizyness a chicken, as is the Chewa custom, and took the second wife. Later he added two more wives to his family.

To keep matters equitable, Mr Banda enhances his sexual drive by using an aphrodisiac called *vubwi*, a root that he grinds into powder. He now has nine children, six with Lizyness, who appears to have accepted the arrangement, and says she is fortunate to have a husband who handles his affairs well and spends two days with each wife. About the other wives, she says, "We go to fetch water together, we sit and chat, and even groom each other's hair."

Florence Soko, wife number three, who already had experience of a polygamous marriage, says she met Mr. Banda at a Chewa cultural festival, was smitten by his drumming, and fell in love. Tyness Tembo, the fourth wife, knew she would be joining three others, but points out advantages. "My friends [the other wives] will look after my child when I am away."

The wives are adamant that there will not be a fifth wife. "The compound hasn't got enough room for a fifth house," said Florence, "and besides, Mr. Banda has already divided his land into four plots for us to cultivate." Banda, meanwhile, is satisfied, "Now I don't have any lovers outside my home. I have all I need."

In towns and cities, traditional medicine for the average Zambian sits comfortably alongside its Western counterpart, with both being used to treat ailments that may range from tick fever to malaria. In rural areas the traditional healer plays a much more important role and may be the only source of medical help for many miles. He will either have inherited his skills from an older family member or have served an apprenticeship with a recognized practitioner. Either way, his practice is unregulated, requiring no qualifications, and has links with witchcraft and spirits.

A visit to any Zambian market will reveal the practice of geophagy, or clay eating, among the female population. Next to the cabbages, tomatoes, sweet potatoes, and the plethora of other vegetables and fruit that cover the market stalls are the vendors of clay soil, more usually for pregnant women but liked by most women. Soil from termite mounds is a particular favorite, soothing morning sickness and preventing the build-up of saliva. Mildly addictive, the ancient practice of clay eating is now thought by scientists to promote digestive health and lower food toxicity.

To date in Zambia there is no formal integration of traditional medicine and modern biomedicine, and any hint of witchcraft by traditional healers is likely to be shown little tolerance by a Christian government.

BAPTISM
It is usual to have a baby baptized or christened according to Roman Catholic and Anglican traditions. The child is becoming a new member of God's family, and those present—family members and godparents who will support them in bringing up the infant in a

Christian way of life—are there to witness the event. It is an important occasion for Zambian churchgoers, and everyone will wear their best clothes. There may be a reception after the baptism.

The Baptist and Pentecostal Churches hold a special dedication service in which the baby is presented to God. The celebrant says prayers over the child, and the parents formally ask for God's blessing on him or her.

With the growth of Pentecostal Churches in Zambia, baptism by immersion is widespread. The difference between the two forms of baptism rests on the fact that baptism by immersion involves young people and adults, who are making an informed choice, including repentance. It is a significant occurrence in the life of a Church member, and much celebrating follows. Smaller churches without a baptism pool will use rivers and lakes in which to conduct the ceremony.

The baby is formally given a name at birth, and afterward, if baptism takes place, he or she is likely to be given a Christian name at the ceremony. The birth name may be that of an ancestor, or indicate a sentiment associated with the birth, such as Bupe (gift, in Bemba), Misozi (tear, in Nyanja), Lelato (love, in Lozi) or Mapenzi (trouble, in Tonga). With 380,000 children orphaned by AIDS, and 85,000 living with HIV, perhaps it is not surprising that the names Masiye (orphan) and Chisonis (sadness) are common. Pity the children called Mulangani (punish me) and Chilumba (my brother's grave)!

FUNERALS
Funerals in Zambia are similar to those in Europe or the US, with family, colleagues, and friends visiting

the home of the surviving spouse to offer condolences. Whereas in Western societies the visitors come and go fairly quickly, in Zambia they may stay for a number of hours. This is regarded as good manners, and a sign of respect to the deceased. Men and women mourn separately, with the men taking up a position outside the house, usually under large canvas awnings, often borrowed from the defense forces (in towns) or hired, while the women sit inside. The men tend to sit stoically, chatting softly, while the women cry and wail loudly—this is particularly noticeable when a new arrival enters the room they are sitting in. It is *de rigueur* for women to wear a brightly patterned *chitenge* (wrap-around skirt) over their normal clothes.

Food and drink (sometimes beer) are provided, with the mourners being regarded as guests. All the women assist with the cooking, and food is taken to the men outside. If the night is cold a large log fire is lit, or *mbaula* (charcoal braziers) are brought out. A choir from the deceased's church may arrive and sing to the gathering. Close family and friends may stay at the house overnight. Increasingly, in urban areas and certainly among the wealthy, the services of a funeral director will be used, while in the rural areas the body is prepared according to traditional practices.

The burial is a somber affair that will take place only when all the relatives are present. The mourners will walk to the interment place or travel in cars and trucks. The singing of religious songs marks the way. At the burial site the coffin is often open so that mourners may file by and view the body. The coffin is lowered into the ground, and is often cemented over to stop thieves desecrating it by stealing clothing or personal items. The grave mound is banked up, with family members helping, and wreaths are placed on it. A memorial service with the placing of a headstone may take place a year after the burial.

Cremations are rare, despite overcrowding in the council cemeteries and the high cost of interment in private burial grounds. Many Zambian Christians believe that cremation is a pagan ritual, and unethical; furthermore, burial is part and parcel of Zambian life. The Hindu crematorium to the west of Lusaka has long been the only such facility.

The AIDS epidemic with which Zambia has been struggling for more than thirty years has had a devastating effect upon the population and on individual families. Financially, the loss of a loved one can be a huge burden. Mourning and attending funerals has become a feature of life in Zambia: every family and workplace has suffered bereavement, and attendance at the mourning and the burial is regarded as essential. Workers are readily given time off, with a subsequent heavy loss of productivity. In 2015, around 1.2 million people were living with AIDS, and with an adult prevalence rate of 12.9 percent there will be many more difficult days ahead, despite the greatly improved access to retroviral treatment.

"SEXUAL CLEANSING"

In rural parts of Zambia a process of "sexual cleansing" or "purification" of the widow or widower takes place after the death of a spouse. The idea is that sexual intercourse will chase away the spirit of the dead from the living partner. In Bemba this practice is referred to as *kupyanika*, and in Tonga as *kusalazya*, and it is carried out by a relative of the dead spouse. Failure to undertake it is thought to bring bad luck, and those who refuse to undergo it risk being cursed and despised by the village. Naturally, the surviving spouses agree to unprotected sex out of fear, even though the HIV/AIDS status of the person performing the ritual is unknown. Of course, if the survivor is HIV positive, the disease will transmit to the "cleanser."

A widow is inherited in what is called a levirate marriage, where she will marry the person who performed the "sexual cleansing." This archaic practice, which regards a woman as a piece of property, is widely condemned as barbaric in Zambia, and is outlawed by the government and chiefs.

Today "cleansing" of the remaining spouse is still widespread, even among the urban educated, but alternative rituals are performed. The person to be cleansed may bathe in water that has been infused with roots and herbs or, alternatively, drink an herbal concoction that has been put into a traditional soft drink, such as from the *munkoyo* plant. A widow may be given a string of colored beads to be worn on her wrist or waist until it disintegrates; white beads are included in the string, and are believed to chase away the spirit of the deceased.

Flour (*mpemba*), either mealie meal (cornflour) or cassava flour, may be thrown in the faces of relatives of the deceased; this is an act of blessing, a wish that they may be bestowed with the favor of God, though formerly it was thrown to drive away spirits.

In some rural areas alternative cleansing may be done by "thigh-brushing," when a half-naked woman (if she is to be cleansed) slides over the thighs of a half-naked man (*kucuta* in Tonga), or vice-versa if the man is to be cleansed. For modesty's sake, a *chitenge* covers those engaged in the cleansing. For some, the cleansing is achieved by shaving their scalps before the rest of the mourners leave the funeral house, and relatives may also do the same.

The widow, after cleansing, is expected to wear black mourning attire for at least a year, unlike a widower. Unless the husband has specifically left a will to the contrary, it is likely that all the family's assets will be taken from her and her children. The family may regard the widow as responsible for the death of her husband, even if the death was from natural causes or as a result of an accident. Retribution is needed, and the female in-laws particularly are seen to be at the forefront of the property grabbing. Despite the "Intestate Succession Act 1989," which makes for a division of the estate according to percentages, women are subjected to patriarchal customary laws and continue to face discrimination in inheritance laws, with witchcraft emerging as a major impediment as far as claiming their rights is concerned.

MARRIAGE

According to UNICEF (2016), 6 percent of girls in Zambia are married by the time they are fifteen, and 31 percent by the age of eighteen, these figures largely reflecting customs in the rural areas. Here the initiation practices prepare a girl for marriage once she reaches puberty, and many parents see marriage as an opportunity to benefit financially from the bride price they will receive for their daughter. In March 2016 the government adopted a five-year national action plan to end child marriages, which are particularly common in eastern Zambia, and ensure that the opportunities for a decent education are available to all.

For those who wish to marry, there are a number of important steps to follow, although, with seventy-two ethnic groups, there are variations. These traditional stages must be observed before the actual marriage ceremony, and mark a gradation of acceptance by both families. When a couple in a steady relationship wishes to get married, the prospective bridegroom will set the procedure in motion by appointing a trustworthy friend and confidant (*shibukombe* in Bemba, *thenga* in Tumbuka), who acts as an intermediary between his friend and the young woman's family. The first step the *shibukombe* must undertake is to carry a symbol or expression of his friend's intent to her parents—the token (*insalamu* in Bemba). Ordinarily this may be a small amount of cash, and in return the *shibukombe* may be given a very simple meal to take back to the man. By undertaking these straightforward acts, the families indicate they acknowledge the intention of their children. At this point, the man may give a ring to the woman as a way of officially declaring his love and their intention to marry.

The time up to the wedding day for the couple is known as *nkobekela*, the period of official engagement. From now on, the families have officially accepted the relationship, and it is regarded as a time when the pair can get to know each other better.

The final step is the *amatebeto*, where the woman's family prepares a feast for the man and his family. His fiancée has no part to play in this. This is an important stage, symbolizing the impending union between the two families, and is an opportunity for them to socialize. At the same time it allows the man's family to learn something of the food culture of their potential daughter-in-law—this is particularly important if she is from a different part of Zambia. The women from the bride's family proceed slowly in a line, head-carrying the food into the reception place, amid melodious singing and hip-shaking dancing, before putting the large bowls down. Each woman then crouches or lies down, one after another, and pushes the food with her head toward the groom-to-be; she should not look up, as this would be disrespectful. Finally, when all the dishes have been brought in and each displayed, the man's hands and feet are washed and the women who brought the food retire to their own homes. Now the man's family eat the new delicacies that they may not have encountered before.

Before the wedding day, the *lobola*, or dowry, must be given by the man to his fiancée's parents. Some regard the *lobola* as the premium to be exacted for owning something, with the amount and kind varying from tribe to tribe. Others say that it is a compensatory measure for the loss of their daughter. Cattle-owning tribes such as the Tonga, Ila, and Lozi prefer the dowry in cattle, or their cash equivalent, while others, particularly in rural areas, traditionally give iron tools, beads, or cloth. The amount to be given will have been negotiated by the *shibukombe* and the bride's family; it is very much dependent upon her educational attainment and, to a much lesser degree, her morals and family values.

The importance of educational attainment in the dowry stakes might be seen as an incentive to keep girls at school longer and to ensure that they do well. The parents are seen to get a return on their "investment." For others, *lobola* is a padlock that keeps an unhappy wife in a home where she is regarded as a personal possession.

A kitchen party or bridal shower follows for the bride-to-be, and is an opportunity for the women of the two families and friends to meet each other socially while presenting gifts. This is a Western import, and is seen as a way of equipping the couple's household, the quality of gifts having risen dramatically from plastic bowls and wooden cooking sticks to a whole range of appliances. The event has

become increasingly significant in urban Zambia, and there are a number of luxurious venues that cater for these—popular with women, the kitchen party is an opportunity to wear their finest clothes, dance, and drink a great deal, away from their husbands. According to the WHO (World Health Organization), Zambian women are the world's heaviest drinkers, with 41.2 percent binge-drinking at least once a week. Zambian men weigh in at sixth place in the binge stakes, with 48.1 percent imbibing heavily once a week.

Assuming the *lobola* has been given to the bride's parents, within the village context the couple are now considered married, and what follows is the *ubwinga* (Bemba) ceremony. This takes place at night, and includes initiation rites for the bride and groom. The *ukulula* (Bemba) ceremony takes place the next day, when the bride and groom sit on a woven cane mat to receive members of both families. This may go on for hours in large families.

The next step for those living in urban areas is the wedding day itself, with a church wedding favored by most. But before this takes place the bride-to-be undertakes further instruction referred to as *ukushanina na bwinga* (Bemba) the night before the church or registry wedding.

A church wedding and the reception afterwards are notoriously expensive, with a guest list of many hundreds. Money for this may be collected from family and friends, but wealthy parents take this as an opportunity to show how well off they are, and indeed how well connected they are, with an array of political figures making an appearance.

Everyone in Zambia is aware of the importance of the appropriate wedding outfits for the bride and groom and the best men and bridesmaids. It is never one best man, a couple of bridesmaids, and a flower girl. The line-up is long, and it is important that the bridal party make a splendid entrance into the reception room. There's loud music, dance music, perhaps some rhumba from the DRC. Azonto from Ghana makes for a real arrival. Whatever the case, it's synchronized steps, hips gyrating, and knees bending. Photographs, even at the most humble wedding, are vital, and most weekends you can see wedding groups posing in front of city flowers and foliage.

Under the Marriage Act, a man having more than one wife is guilty of bigamy and liable to a sentence of up to five years' imprisonment. It is perhaps not surprising that some men will contract marriage under customary law, since under that law there is no penalty for additional marriages. Polygamy is most common among the Tonga and the Mambwe and Namwanga of northern Zambia and the Chewa of eastern Zambia.

Men who have contracted a legal marriage under the Marriage Act are still likely to enter into adulterous affairs. Extra "wives" and "side-chicks" (girlfriends) are almost expected by women, and it is rare to see a married couple out together in the evening. It is more usual for the wife to be at home with the children while her husband, cronies, and girlfriends are out on the town—she would, of course, still be expected to have food on the table when the wanderer returns!

chapter four

MAKING
FRIENDS

Zambians are sociable. A particular feature of
the friendship patterns that exist today are the
relationships between the once-warring Bemba and
Ngoni; the Lozi and the Tonga and Ila; and the Lozi
and the Ndebele of Zimbabwe.

These relationships or cousinships are very
important, no more so than between the Bemba and
the Ngoni. These tribal relationships came into being
after the establishment of colonial rule, when young
people migrated to seek work in towns and found
themselves far away from their homelands. Thrown
together, they were in situations where it was found
to be beneficial to let old tribal animosities and
rancor go, and establish what are called "joking
relationships." This banter between groups who
were formerly hostile to each other now provides
for functional collaboration between them.

Weddings and funerals are the best places to
see this tribal interplay, though President Kenneth
Kaunda, the first president of the republic, did
referee a Bemba *v.* Ngoni soccer match in 2002!
When President Michael Sata, who was a Bemba,
died in October 2014, thousands of his Ngoni
"cousins" came out to do *mgubo* at the official
mourning to celebrate his life. This practice involves

sprinkling white powder (maize meal, talcum powder, or crushed lime) on anyone thought to be Bemba. This particular *mgubo* involved a female Ngoni Member of Parliament who sprinkled powder on a police officer on duty at the Mulungushi International Conference Centre, where the body viewing was taking place. All good-humored fun, which President Sata would have approved of—he had commented that he could not declare Chipata to be a city because easterners (Ngonis) were backward!

SOCIALIZING

Working with Zambians provides many opportunities for mixing and getting to know people well, and, rest assured, a Zambian knows where to go on an afternoon or evening out! There are a great many bars

and eateries. For those expatriates who in the course
of their work in aid agencies or in the diplomatic
corps do not meet many Zambians, there are many
events, associations, clubs, and classes in all the
large cities, especially Lusaka. Visiting a church
for a Sunday service is always a warm, inviting
experience, and the Lusaka Family Church, the
Eternal Life Fellowship, and the Miracle Life Family
Church are good places to meet local people and
their families. There are birdwatching clubs, animal
welfare societies, health and sporting clubs, music
societies, and, of course, the Alliance Française.

Zambians are friendly and generous to strangers,
but that cordiality seldom extends to home
hospitality. You are unlikely to meet the family
unless you invite them all to a function at your home
or a day out somewhere. Guests at family weddings
and funeral mourners can make excellent company,
and much can be learned from a well-informed
commentator.

FORMS OF ADDRESS

Bemba and Nyanja are the two languages spoken the
most in Zambia: Bemba in the Copperbelt, Luapula,
Muchinga, and Northern Provinces; and Nyanja in
Lusaka and Eastern Provinces.

Zambian adults address each other by their
surnames, so it's Mr. Mulenga (Bemba), Mr. Mwanza
(Nyanja), Mr. Sitali (Lozi), or Mr. Muntanga
(Tonga). The surname indicates the origins of that
person, as it often does in other parts of the world,
and a Zambian knows someone's background from
the name. Mutale, Kunda, Chungu, Musonda,
and Sata are Bemba; Banda, Mvula, Jere, and

Sakala are Ngoni; Ikasaya, Monde, Mwangala, and Mwanangombe are Lozi; and Muleya, Himpyali, Chilala, and Hakasanke are Tonga.

Addressing or referring to an adult by his or her first name is regarded as impolite, and is reserved only for long-time close friends, children, and adolescents. If you are close to the person you may use the term for father or mother of their child: for example, in Bemba it might be *Bashi* Bupe (Father of Bupe) or *Bana* Bupe (Mother of Bupe) and in Nyanja, *Atate* Dalitso (Father of Dalitso) or *Amake* Dalitso (Mother of Dalitso).

Some groups have gender signifiers in their surnames, among them the Namwanga from Muchinga Province and the Mambwe and Lungu from Northern Province. A man's surname begins with "Si," and a woman's with "Na." The daughter of a man named Sinkamba has the surname Nakamba.

In Zambia there isn't a precise corresponding word for "Hi," "Hello," or "Good-bye," and instead the general greeting is an enquiry after a person's health: "*Muli shani*?" ("How are you?" in Bemba), which may be abbreviated to "*Shani*" in informal situations. In Nyanja it would be "*Muli bwanji*," or "*Bwanji*." A person replies by confirming that they are "*Ndi bwino*" or in Nyanja "*Ndili bwino*" (I'm well." "Good afternoon" becomes "*Mwatandeleni*" in Bemba, assuming you are greeting someone from a resting situation, and "*Mwabombeni*" if you are working; in Nyanja the phrase "*Mwachoma bwanji*" is used.

A Zambian will refer to a language as being "deep," meaning that the grammar, phrasing, and vocabulary are from the tribal heartland. Someone speaking "deep Bemba" would typically be from Kasama District in the Northern Province, while someone speaking "deep Nyanja" would be from Chipata District in the Eastern

Province. This would be instantly recognizable, since the Bemba and Nyanja spoken in other areas have been corrupted, and slang may be used.

GREETINGS

There is a degree of protocol attached to handshaking, with the situation and participants determining the type. Men and women may shake hands upon meeting, but it is also common to see each make a greeting by standing at a distance, clasping their own hands in front of their chests, and bowing their heads with a smile. Alternatively, the two parties may bow and gently pat their chests with the right hand in recognition of the other person. It is not unusual to greet work colleagues on a daily basis with a handshake and a general question about their health. This may seem an interminable chore in a large gathering but is generally a joyful show of camaraderie and unity.

When greeting a relative, particularly an older person, it is more respectful to first cup your hands and then clap two or three times, bending your knee, almost curtseying, while asking, "How are you?" The handshake may then take place, to be followed by more cupped handclapping. In the event of meeting someone particularly important, the right hand is extended to receive the handshake and is supported by the left hand, which holds the arm – this movement is accompanied by a bowing of the head and may be used by opportunistic social climbers and job seekers!

Someone who wants to demonstrate extra affection may well use the two-handed handshake. Here the additional effort of including the other hand lends itself to a show of greater emotion and sentiment—popular with politicians! Finally, when two good friends meet the "African Handshake" may be used, in which the traditional handshake is switched into a friendly hand-grasp and back again to a shake, maybe ending with a flourish, where the fingertips click as the hands are withdrawn.

THE OPPOSITE SEX

In Zambia it is unusual to see couples holding hands or kissing. Affection of any kind is ordinarily left for private moments, unless you happen to be a wealthy European or American, in which case persuasive dalliance may take matters further. It does seem to be the case that overweight, late-middle-aged, white men can make friends with young, attractive Zambian girls who are pert and coquettish, with a ready twinkle in their eyes. It is impossible to feel old here!

There are many stories of "sugar daddies" and their female counterparts, "sugar mommies," in Zambia. The chasing of wealthy, older, married men by young girls for material and monetary gains has long been an issue, and as school and university fees rise and family structures are broken (largely through the AIDS pandemic), the problem is likely to increase. Of equally long standing, but less visible, are the wealthy older women who seek solace and intimacy with young men.

In fact, there is a danger that the male outsider can become engulfed in the whirl of social enterprise, where it is regarded as fairly normal to have a little extramarital affair. When he should be gasping for a cup of tea, hating noisy pubs, or preferring a relaxing night in to a night on the town, he has slipped into a hedonist's quagmire of turpitude. For a late night out, it is always best to carry the bare minimum—just enough cash, including the taxi fare home, and a cheap cell phone rather than a smartphone. And note that it's rarely wise to go out alone.

As in most countries, girls should always go out with friends and keep a watchful eye on each other. Look after your purse, mind your drinks if you are on the dance floor, and take a friend to the bathroom with you. Zambian men are proud of their masculinity, and their upbringing makes them confident rather than overbearing. They are generous when they have money, and will always expect to pick up the tab when dating. In the cities, a Zambian man is keen to impress—debit and credit cards—check!

MIXED-RACE RELATIONSHIPS

Aside from casual trysts—between aging foreigners (who have left their wives at home) and accommodating local women—interracial dating and marriage really does work. There have been many successful marriages and a few that have failed, generally when the couple have returned to the husband's home country and the wife has been unable to settle. At the same time, Zambian men have happily married women from outside the country who have become fully integrated into society and the role of bringing up a family in Zambia.

Where once, many years ago, Zambians were ill disposed to mixed-race relationships, and a couple in a public place might hear muttering, today such arrangements are accepted, and families are content to see that their children are happy. Modern Zambia has moved on, and embraces heterosexual interfaith, intercultural, and interracial relationships where love, compatibility, and respect matter the most.

LENDING MONEY

Credit in Zambia is known as *nkongole*, and is pretty much a fact of life, especially toward the end of the month. "Can you borrow me five pin?" can be translated as "Can you lend me five thousand kwacha?" The words "borrowing" and "lending" tend to be interchangeable in Zambia, but whichever is used, to a visitor from outside the country, this is generally a request for financial help—in other words, a gift. The intention of the person asking may be honorable, and he or she may well intend to pay back the money, but the problem is: when? In the circumstances, it is always good to be able to oblige, but to have no expectation of a return.

CONVERSATION

It is always good manners to greet and shake hands before making any attempt at conversation, regardless of how many people are in the meeting room. You are introducing yourself to everyone, and thereby securing your right to be in the gathering and your entitlement to speak when necessary. Joining a group of friends is just the same—shake hands, irrespective of whether the person is known to you or not.

Small talk is always an appropriate opener. There's always soccer, local or international; satellite TV is widespread, and everyone is up to date with the scores and the latest moves in the "transfer window." Politics are openly discussed, and everyone has an opinion. Newspapers are widely read, and political happenings on the radio and TV are mulled over and analyzed, especially in the pubs and clubs. The population is comparatively small, and everybody seems to know a politician, a musician, or a top civil servant personally and can shed light on what is going on. There is always much to discuss: the state of the roads, the political parties, fuel prices, and corruption.

It is never a good idea to introduce the subject of AIDS into a conversation, since practically all Zambian families have suffered bereavement and are coping with its consequences. Religion can be a difficult topic for the unbeliever, and many Zambians would be surprised to find an atheist in their midst.

INVITATIONS

City weddings, christenings, and kitchen parties are big invitation-only events, and you will need to plan your wardrobe carefully. Men should wear suits, as most Zambians aspire to the old adage of "A gentleman knows no weather." A suit, collar, and tie are *de rigueur* for these occasions, even when the temperature is in the sweltering nineties in the shade and there's a possibility of passing out from the heat.

Women must be dressed "up to the nines." To shine and sparkle is everything. Seize the opportunity to look your best from head to toe. There are some South African fashion outlets in the shopping malls, and there's an increasing number of young Afrocentric or Western designers, especially in Lusaka, who can readily create something just for you.

Food at such occasions is usually an al fresco buffet meal, with a huge variety of meats, vegetables, and carbs. Washing hands precedes the meal, as *nshima* (stiff, maize-meal porridge; see page 99) will be served, and is ordinarily eaten using the fingers—so hands are washed after the meal as well. Cutlery is normally provided for foreign guests. Hearty eaters should be warned that desserts are somewhat rare.

Speeches tend to go on, as everyone feels that they have something to share, regardless of the program. The MC can often be the most loquacious, and sometimes this part of the proceedings can resemble a scene from *Lord of the Flies*, in which whoever can get to the microphone (conch shell) has an entitlement to speak.

Always try to be on time, as this will be expected of you as a *mzungu*. When leaving, it is of course important to thank your host for the invitation and hospitality.

chapter five

THE ZAMBIANS AT HOME

A ROOF OVER YOUR HEAD

It is much easier to find a place to live in a rural village than in a town: simply build your own house. Many years ago a traditional hut consisted of a round, wooden framework of woven sticks plastered over with a sticky mix of clay and straw. The structure had woven roof trusses rising to the center, over which thatch, usually from mopane grass, was spread.

These huts, situated in a family group, were temporary, and reflected the agricultural practices that were widespread, namely the *chitemene* system (shifting, or slash-and-burn cultivation). Today's village structures are far more substantial, with baked brick walls and thatched roofs. Clay from termite mounds is highly prized, as it makes the strongest

bricks, when mixed with water. The bricks are shaped in wooden molds, dried in a shady place, and then built into a kiln. A twenty-four-hour firing is enough, then the kiln is dismantled and the bricks are used for building. They are laid on a raised floor to prevent water entering during the rainy season.

The houses are grouped together, each family having a grass-screened pit latrine and washing area. The men and boys eat in their own *insaka* (Bemba for "place to gather") and another *insaka* is used for cooking and for the women to get together in. A *ntamba*, a raised wooden drying area for pots and plates, is situated next to the cooking *insaka*. The area around each house is swept daily by the women and girls using a *cheswa* (Bemba), a grass brush.

The houses and dwellings in the towns and cities are not as homogeneous, and a roof over your head here might mean living in a shanty compound, a purpose-built "site and service scheme," a run-down apartment block, a civil servant's house, an old mine worker's house complete with *stoep* (veranda), or one of the new out-of-town residential areas. The reality is, though, that most of the population live in shanty

compounds in intense poverty on less than US $1.25 a day. The dearth of decent, affordable housing is critical, with 70 percent of urban residents not connected to the main sewage systems and 60 percent without access to public water systems in their homes. Middle managers might find themselves living in what are nominally servants' quarters because of the high rent—in Lusaka a three-bedroom apartment in a good area might cost as much as 20,000 KMW (US $2,000) a month, with prices higher in Kalundu, Leopards Hill, or New Kasama— almost twice the cost of renting in Cape Town, South Africa. With the shortage of good-quality housing at the higher end of the market, there has been a growth of gated communities and modern cluster-style neighborhoods, some aimed at Zambians who work abroad and wish to maintain a foothold in the country. Outside Lusaka the rents fall, but of course there are fewer job opportunities and lengthy tedious commutes for those working in the city.

You can secure a plot of land and build your own house. It sounds simple, but the urban peripheries are littered with concrete floor slabs and half-finished "wall fences" put up by those who tried. The wall fence is a ubiquitous presence in Zambia, mostly topped with razor wire or at the very least shards of glass. Security for all is an issue; homeowners put burglar bars on all the windows and install security lighting, and those who can afford it subscribe to a private rapid response team.

Mortgage finance is expensive, with interest rates ranging between 22.5 and 27.5 percent. At the same time, transaction costs are high at more than 5 percent of the total loan amount, and the deposit required is as much as 20 percent. Loan repayment terms of two to fifteen years also make obtaining a mortgage difficult.

Sixty percent of the population are projected to live in urban areas by 2050, and there is enormous pressure on towns and cities for land, houses, and the basic provision of water supply, solid waste management, and sanitation.

DAILY LIFE

A mother and daughter in a Zambian village work extremely hard. They rise as early as 5:00 a.m. to light a fire, in order to heat water for washing for the men and boys when they get up. They sweep inside and outside the house, and fetch water from the well or river, which may be some distance away. They wash the dishes from the previous meal, and cook the breakfast—usually maize-meal porridge. Afterwards, the daughter is expected to care for her younger siblings, do the laundry, and collect firewood with her mother and other women. Foraging for wild fruits, roots, and insects in season brings extra food into the household. The girls and women will also catch small fish in shallow water, using baskets, while the men and boys use nets. During the planting and harvesting

periods they work in the fields with other family members. There used to be no time for a girl to be in school, but in the last forty years the numbers enroled in primary school have risen steeply—though, as we have seen, there is an alarming dropout rate in eastern areas, where some are taken as very young brides.

Men and boys live a much more privileged existence, and most of the boys attend school. Their work around the family home involves repairing the property and cutting down trees for wood that the women and girls will collect when dry. The boys catch wild birdsfor food, using snares or catapults, or smearing branches with sticky birdlime made from wild fruits, to stop the birds flying away once they've perched. In areas where animal husbandry is important, the boys look after the animals as they wander through the bush. In fishing communities, the men might spend time repairing their nets (sadly, in many areas, mosquito nets are being used for fishing instead) or dugout canoes, and drying the catch.

Village children play traditional games when time allows. Lacking modern electronic games, toys, and TV, the children in the village, and indeed much of Zambia, make their own toys and entertainment. Wire cars, clay dolls, rope, an *icimpombwa*—a ball made of rolled-up plastic bags or cloth tied together with string or bark fibre—and the omnipresent tire make for hours of fun.

Girls in a Bemba-speaking village, when time allows, play traditional games such as *ukuteya ichibale* (a game with colored beads), *ukubuta* (make-believe cooking), and *ukushana* (dancing). Boys play soccer with an *icimpombwa* and *isolo*, a board game.

Children of the well-to-do in cities and towns have a lifestyle comparable to those in the West—

smartphones, tablets, satellite TV, and private schools, thus escaping the overcrowded classrooms, lack of facilities, and poor teaching associated with state schools. They have fewer household chores to do—such families have servants for these tasks, as well as for gardening and driving the children around. The parents are probably working, joining the commuter traffic lines into the cities, with most businesses and offices opening at 8:00 a.m. and finishing at 5:00 p.m. Extended family members pick up the routine childcare duties and often the shopping.

Breastfeeding babies in public is regarded as normal, and it is never a good idea for the outsider to stare. No place is improper to a feeding mother, be it shopping mall, restaurant, or bus.

FOOD AND DRINK

Maize meal is the staple grain of Zambia, and its importance to the Zambian people cannot be overstated. Its price has always had enormous political implications for the country, and the government has in the past stepped in to stabilize prices by releasing cheap grain from the Food Reserve Agency to the millers.

The staple food, *nshima*, is made by grinding grain (usually maize kernels) into fine flour, to which boiling water is added to make a thick porridge. This is spooned from the pot using a large wooden cooking stick or scoop, and served, blisteringly hot, on plates, always with some kind of relish including onions and

tomatoes. *Nshima* is ordinarily eaten twice a day, starting with breakfast, when there are leftovers from the night before. Cassava, sorghum, and millet may also be ground to produce flour for *nshima*.

An alternative breakfast might be roasted or dried cassava with peanuts, or sweet potatoes and peanuts. *Samp*, lightly crushed maize kernels, might be served boiled with milk and sugar or added to sour milk.

Traditional green vegetables that are likely to be used as a relish in many homes include *kalembula* (sweet potato leaves), *katapa* (cassava leaves), *umulembwe* (okra leaves), *chimpapila* (bean leaves), and *chibabwa* (pumpkin leaves). These are seasonal when sold fresh, but can be bought dried in all the markets. In the village, of course, the ability to dry produce in the absence of electricity for refrigerators and freezers is vital. The tubers and fruits of the plants are eaten either fresh or dried. Cabbage, broccoli rabe, spinach, and kale, more recently introduced leafy vegetables, are boiled with a dash of cooking oil, as are the traditional greens. Pounded peanuts are added to vegetables to provide additional flavor and food value, in a dish called *ifisashi* (Bemba).

Local fruits are collected from the miombo woodland through the dry season until December. There can't be a village or a home in Zambia that doesn't have a mango tree providing shade and fruit, though this is hardly indigenous. Avocado and

guava trees are more recent additions to the village and town landscape, and swarm with children in season.

At the onset of the rains, mushrooms appear in the woodland and every villager makes haste to gather them. Roadside vendors appear with mushrooms like small umbrellas, all colors and sizes, waiting to be fried with onions and tomatoes and served with *nshima*.

CHIKANDA, OR AFRICAN POLONY

There are over 26,000 species of orchid, and those found in areas of northern Zambia and its neighbors have tubers that make a delicious meat substitute. Also known as the "Zambian sausage," *chikanda*, made from tubers, is a delicacy served with *nshima* as a main course, and is entirely meat-free!

The brown or white tubers are in such demand in Zambia that there is evidence that wild orchid populations are being severely depleted, and that the tubers on sale are smaller than they used to be. Five-star hotels have joined the humblest street markets in having *chikanda* on their menus, and this has led to Zambia having to import orchid tubers.

Chilemba (made from dried beans) is the usual accompaniment for *nshima* in many state boarding schools. Soaked overnight and allowed to boil with cooking oil, onions, and tomatoes, this cheap source of protein has filled many a hungry stomach. Meat is a luxury for many families, and killing a village chicken is saved for a special occasion. Protein requirements are likely to be met by what is available in the countryside.

Bush Protein

Zambian bush protein is varied, and might fly, crawl, or walk, and have two, four, or six legs. Most birds are regarded as meat, and are therefore liable to find their way into the pot, while giant mole rats—which are particularly evident when the land is cleared and fires lit as the new planting season arrives—are dug out of the ground. Regretfully, most Zambians enjoy eating game meat, and poaching has become a serious problem in many of the National Parks. *Inswa* (flying ants) are caught as they leave the anthills at the beginning of the rains. They have their wings removed before being sun-dried and fried with a little salt before eating or storing in airtight containers. One often sees small bowls of dried *inswa* at social gatherings. *Finkubala* (caterpillars) are a Bemba delicacy, found in much of the country. Also known as mopane worms, the name taken from the type of woodland where they are found, these are the larvae of the emperor moth. They can be dried, then eaten as a crunchy snack, or cooked, or rehydrated for a softer texture and cooked with onions and tomatoes.

Green grasshoppers known as *shongonono* are found in fields and on cultivated patches of land and are available from January to March, during the rainy season. They are caught by hand, their wings removed, then fried and served as a relish with *nshima*. Cicadas and bee larvae are also important sources of protein.

The forests of northwestern Zambia are very important for honey and beeswax production using traditional bark hives. These are hung high in the trees, which protects them from army ants and honey badgers, and wild swarms soon take over. After about a year the honeycomb inside is ready for harvesting and the hive is lowered. The bees are driven to one end of the hive by smoke, allowing the beekeeper to harvest the comb from the other end. The residue after the beeswax has been washed can be used to make honey beer, a popular drink in the villages.

Zambians love their meat, and aside from the restaurants offering every conceivable cut of beef, pork, chicken, and goat, there are many kiosks barbecuing T-bone and ribeye steaks on *mbaula* (small charcoal braziers). No part of the animal is wasted, and chicken heads, feet, and intestines might be found in a freezer cabinet alongside pigskin and fat. A particular favorite part of the chicken is the gizzard, which, when thoroughly washed, with the hard skin inside removed, and fried with lots of garlic, is tasty addition to the dinner table.

Fresh fish can be easily bought in supermarkets with Kariba bream, *kapenta*, and Nile perch from Lake Tanganyika being very popular. Communities along the Zambezi, in the Lukanga Swamps, and the great Lake Bangweulu wetlands have long had a fish diet, with much being dried or smoked for preservation. *Kapenta* are small, freshwater sardines that are caught at night in Lake Tanganyika and Lake Kariba. Using fishing rigs fitted with bright mercury lights, the fishermen follow schools of *kapenta* and scoop them up with large nets as they rise close to the surface, attracted by the lights. These may be sold fresh, but larger quantities are sun-dried, packed into sacks, and taken to be sold throughout the country. The *kapenta* are washed and soaked in boiling water for about fifteen minutes, drained, dried, and fried in oil with the omnipresent onions and tomatoes. Rich in protein and vitamin B12, *kapenta* are found in storage jars in most Zambian pantries.

Local Brews

Most villages have brewers—usually women, skilled in the making of traditional nonalcoholic and alcoholic drinks. *Munkoyo*, perhaps Zambia's favorite nonalcoholic beverage, is made from maize meal and the shredded, dried roots of the *munkoyo* plant. Porridge is made and left overnight to ferment before being strained and boiled with additional water. Other nonalcoholic drinks include *thobwa* and *maheu*, traditionally made from millet.

The scourge of many a peaceful village are the alcoholic brews known as *katubi* and *katata* in Bemba. Brewed with similar ingredients, including maize and finger millet, *katubi* is thicker and drunk from a communal container, which is passed around and sucked through a thin metal straw. The brew becomes more potent when hot water is added and the contents of the drinking vessel begin to foam. In many villages and shanty compounds, brewing beer is an important source of income for families needing money for school uniforms, school fees, and general household consumables, and there can be fierce rivalry between brewers.

Kachusu is a particularly potent illicit brew that has had devastating effects in many villages and compounds. Highly addictive, and with an alcohol content of over 45 percent, the spirit is distilled from maize or finger millet and has been linked to long-term psychological and physiological breakdown, with many families struggling through its effects. Shebeens (unlicensed drinking places) selling *kachusu* are found in many townships, and continue to bring misery to their inhabitants.

A major success story for the brewing industry in Zambia has been the commercialization of Chibuku from its humble origins in Kitwe in Zambia's

Copperbelt. First brewed in the 1950s by Max Heinrich, who spotted a market for this traditional artisan beer, this low-cost, opaque product now outsells conventional lager-type beer in Zambia by four to one, and is on track for sale in twelve African countries. Formally sold in dingy taverns throughout Zambia, where it was decanted from large vats into old cooking-oil containers and liter "buckets," Chibuku is now sold in supermarkets, with the traditional "Shake-Shake" product (so called because of the sediment that settles at the bottom) marketed in cartons, and Chibuku Super, thinner and without the sediment, in plastic bottles.

PAYDAY AND MORE

Everyone living in towns and cities seems to be waiting for "the month end," in other words, payday. Everyone has a list of how they think they should spend their wages or salary, but usually the first thing they do is rush out and enjoy themselves. This invariably means that any thoughts about bills, loans to be repaid, and basic needs are pushed to the back burner to await attention later on. It can be all about robbing Peter to pay Paul, or, to be more precise, borrowing from Banda to pay Phiri—but later. Payday is joyous—a time to relax—and the bars, clubs, and restaurants are heaving at this time. Everybody feels rich, and the "good times roll" for a while as the cash is splashed and cares are forgotten.

For the villagers, life is a little different, more leisurely, less to do with mammon (material things) and more to do with maize. Most families have just enough to eat and some to sell or exchange to provide for the family's other needs. The "local" shop is unlikely to sell much more than cooking oil, salt, sugar, laundry soap, candles, matches, carbolic washing soap, and Vaseline; and a trip to town can take days. Many items sold in the villages and the high-density areas are small, repackaged units of basic food items such as salt, sugar, and maize meal and are known as *pamela*, demonstrating the hand-to-mouth existence of many families. Cigarettes have been sold by the "stick" for many years on street corners, outside bars, and in markets.

PUTTING ON THE STYLE

> *"But if a woman have long hair, it is a glory to her:*
> *for her hair is given her for a covering,"*
> 1 Corinthians 11:15 (KJV).

Hair is taken exceedingly seriously in this Christian country, with hair extensions eagerly acquired and the salon and itinerant braiding business booming. It has for years puzzled Westerners that women of Afro-Caribbean origin are able to alter their appearance so rapidly—one day short and curly, the next day long, with waist-length braids, or shoulder-length and straight, or jumbo Marley twists, or …. The business is thriving, with Beyoncé and Rihanna lookalikes in the main cities—long, curly weaves sewn in or glued on, fluffy, crocheted braids, or loose crotchet curls with bangs. The list is endless, and Zambian women are ready to shine.

Newer entrants into the hair business are the Maasai men from Tanzania who have perfected the art of the "twist." Hair extensions are braided in and then twisted into thin threads by repeatedly rolling the threads on a naked thigh! Not quite as exotic as

Top Dressing

For a number of years, our Buizza Hair Salon was the premier ladies' hair business in Zambia, with three salons in Lusaka and one in Kabwe. The ladies in Zambia never underestimate the power of a great hairstyle and, thanks to my wife, we were at the forefront of *au naturel* afro hairdressing, box braids, cornrows, wet looks, and beyond.

We could straighten and relax your hair, condition it and perm it; shampoo and set it; steam it; tint it; hot oil it; and, of course, braid it with hair extensions, referred to as "wigs." We had braiders, shampooers, setters, wet-lookers, and sweepers.

Buizza took Kabwe by storm, and our opening saw us hiring the open-air swimming pool and the appropriately named Third World Disco—with free beer and soft drinks, of course! The day was a huge success, with ladies in line outside like a Black Friday bargain day. We had to get help from Lusaka, and I became a sweeper!

the legend of the female cigar rollers of Cuba, but a reality at about 600 kwacha (US $60) for the finest threads. With three men at work on it, the task, which would take one hairdresser all day, can be completed in about three hours, and the towns have seen a burgeoning of market salons.

For Zambian women, a wedding, kitchen party, graduation ceremony, or birthday party is an opportunity to wear your best clothes, and the traditional *chitenge* outfit takes some beating. At its most basic, the *chitenge* is a length of very colorful patterned cloth, similar to a sarong, that is more usually worn by women wrapped around the

chest or waist as a skirt, or folded as a head-tie. In the village, the *chitenge* is indispensable as a wrap-around overall to protect clothes from dust or dirt, a hair covering (*ichitambala*) to protect from smoke and food odor, and a baby sling (*impapa*, Bemba) worn over one shoulder. It can also be coiled and flattened to make a head cushion (*iqana*, Bemba) to wear beneath heavy containers of water, or firewood.

The Lozi women of the Western Province take social gatherings as opportunities to wear their *musisi* outfits. Thought to have derived from the crinolines worn by the wives of Victorian missionaries and settlers or from Portuguese settlers in Angola, these heavy, very full costumes are given by Lozi parents to their daughters when they reach puberty, and are regarded as heirlooms and keepsakes. The Lozi men have evolved similar attire called *siziba*, consisting of a shirt, a calf-length kilt, sometimes with a matching sleeveless jacket, and a red beret called a *mashushu*.

The first president of the republic, Kenneth Kaunda, was something of a trendsetter when he made safari suits and cravats popular for men. Soon, all the members of the cabinet started to wear the same, and the collar and tie made an exit. The 1991 general election saw a new fashion icon appear in the form of the diminutive second president, Frederick Chiluba, who ushered in an era of sharp suits and patterned silk ties with crisp white shirts. Famous for his Swiss-made, two-inch-high, monogrammed shoes, Chiluba brought male fashion decadence to a high point.

Zambian fashion for women has taken off over the last few years, with young designers making a big impact at the Zambia Fashion Week. Moving away from cheap South African and Chinese imports, the emphasis is on producing bold, bright outfits that offer something different. Often using fabric and trim from the many secondhand-clothes sellers found all over the country, these designers and their tailors bring an alternative couture to the streets.

Second-hand clothing, or *salaula* (Bemba, picking from a pile), has been around since the late 1980s, affording the ordinary Zambian a chance to take part in Western culture. Donated to charities in the West, with some items sold in their thrift and charity shops, much is sorted and baled before being bought by traders for hard cash. These eventually reach Zambia (brought in initially by Lebanese traders) in unique bales of denim jeans, woolen goods, shirts, dresses, shoes, and so on. The downside of this is the impact upon the local textile and garment industry, though it might be said that the growth of the *salaula* business is a direct response to the decline of the industry during the difficult times in the 1980s.

EDUCATION

Though free basic education was introduced in 2002 and entitles a child to primary education from the age of seven to fourteen, which is from Grade 1 to Grade 7, there are a quarter of a million children of primary school age not in school, and 47 percent fail to complete this initial stage. Schools operate a double shift, with the first intake in the morning and a second in the afternoon. Even so, class numbers are very high, with seventy pupils per class being quite usual and facilities and resources virtually nonexistent. Teaching methods are very old-fashioned, with learning by rote and repetition the order of the day. Teachers work from the government handbook, which has basic lesson plans, and these are followed to the letter throughout the country. Poorly qualified and trained teachers tend to reinforce English-language errors with the constant reiteration of grammar or pronunciation mistakes. Since 2014, public primary school pupils from Grade 1 to Grade 4 have been taught in the local language, with English taught as a separate subject.

At the end of Grade 7 pupils take a set of multiple-choice exams, including nonverbal reasoning papers, to judge their suitability for secondary school. Though there has been progress in the opening of secondary schools, there is still a shortage of spaces for students, and the competition is challenging. The cut-off point for selection is determined by the number of spaces, with female students given a lower cut-off point.

Junior secondary education follows in Grades 8 and 9 before further exams to assess fitness for the final

stage of secondary education in a senior secondary school or technical school. At the end of Grade 12, students take School Certificate exams that assess their suitability for tertiary institutions.

There are three public universities in Zambia, and this sector has seen tremendous growth, with nineteen private universities registered. These offer an array of undergraduate, postgraduate, and doctorate programs, but fees have to be paid for tuition and accommodation, with only the exceptional getting government bursaries. It is remarkable how these students manage to find the money to go to university, and the figures show how much education is valued in Zambia. There has also been a growth in the number of private students going to China and Namibia for undergraduate courses and, of course, there are the wealthier who proceed to Australia, South Africa, the UK, and the US.

Technology is slowly making its way into schools, and the government is providing secondary schools with computers and establishing IT suites. The use of touch-screen tablets in primary schools has seen the introduction of a more modern, enquiry-based approach to learning, even in rural schools, where solar power can be harnessed. The ZEdupad, the 32GB tablet, which delivers the entire primary curriculum, was created and developed in Zambia and looks set to become a major player in education in Africa, with additional smartphone access possible as well.

There has been huge growth in the number of private primary and secondary schools offering better facilities and smaller class sizes. Most follow the Zambian curriculum, but a number in the bigger towns and cities follow an American or British system, with specific Key Stages and Cambridge IGCEs and Advanced levels or the International Baccalaureate program.

chapter six

TIME OUT

Zambians have a lot of spare time and a better work/life balance than most North Americans and Europeans. They are naturally sociable, and love doing things in groups. The opportunities for enjoyment are many, ranging from stylish nightclubs with fine dining to seedy shantytown shebeens (pubs).

EATING OUT

Zambians enjoy their *nshima* and relish, but they are quite happy to try something new. There is a huge selection of places to eat, and in Lusaka alone there are more than a hundred. Restaurants from around the world are sprinkled around in the malls and

shopping centers—from Portuguese to Chinese, Japanese to Lebanese— and visitors mustn't forget the street food, the fast-food takeouts, and, of course, the hotels.

Imported seafood is costly, and rather surprisingly some of the Zambian dishes in the high-end hotels are extraordinarily expensive. There are very few vegetarians and vegans in Zambia, by choice, and as a consequence some eateries have rather limited options for them, particularly outside the cities. Generally, restaurant prices are comparable with those in the West. Menus don't usually include the tax (currently 16 percent) or a service charge, and these appear on the bill.

TIPPING

Most restaurants have a 10 percent service charge and therefore, technically, tipping is not required, but Western foreigners are generally expected to tip if the service has been good.

Hairdressers and taxi drivers can be tipped about 5 percent of the cost.

If you are staying in a safari camp it is usual to tip the guides; there is a tip box for general staff.

There is a good selection of beers and wines to go with your meal. Zambian Breweries, formerly Zambia Breweries, was established in the late 1960s and is now owned by ABInBev. Mosi, Castle, Castle Lite, Flying Fish, Carling Black Label, and Eagle (100 percent Zambian ingredients) are lager-type products, all produced in Zambia.

Being close to the vineyards of South Africa, the restaurants have good wine selections, including the excellent Bellingham Old Vine Chenin Blanc 2010 and the Anthonij Rupert Merlot 2006. Wines from Chile, Argentina, France, Spain, and Italy are available.

NIGHTLIFE

Zambia has a thriving nightlife scene, with the weekends particularly lively. Cinemas, some with multiple screens, are found in all the major cities. The Copperbelt and especially Lusaka have both sophisticated clubs and more down-to-earth bars, with live music and DJs providing the backdrop for eating,

drinking, and dancing. You are likely to hear everything from US hip-hop to its Zambian version, Zed HipHop (Zed is the informal name for Zambia), R&B, ZedBeats, reggae, Congolese rhumba, and jazz. For some foreigners, who want to see life in the raw, it's the sleazier the better, and there are plenty of those venues, where it's best to go in a group. You'll find ladies of the night drinking from bottles, the fetid warmth of a crowded dance floor, and instant friends who will want to share your good fortune.

Yes, Zambians like to party! A little-known fact is that if you are a Zambian drinker you are probably drunk at least once a week, according to the WHO.

All the big hotels in Lusaka and the Copperbelt offer after-dark entertainment, those in Livingstone serving up something more ethnic, with traditional dancing, drumming, and music. Here there is always room for you, as a foreigner, to wrap a *chitenge* around your hips, gyrate, thrust, and "shake your booty" as much as you can—the locals love it!

There are cinemas in all the major cities showing the latest releases; 3-D viewing is available in some, and VIP seating in most. Casinos are usually found near hotels, restaurants, and shopping centers, and offer a range of games and slot machines. Lusaka, Kitwe, and Livingstone have casinos with no membership requirements, and these are extremely popular with Chinese clients.

The Lusaka Play House, near the Southern Sun Ridgeway Hotel, is the venue for musical, comedic, and dramatic productions presented by talented local performers and theater groups.

SPORTS

Zambians are both active participants and spectators. Zambian sports owe the copper industry a huge debt of gratitude. Prior to 1998, when privatization took place, the majority state-owned ZCCM (Zambia Consolidated Copper Mines) was the breeding ground for some of the top Zambian sportsmen and women, and sponsored a huge number of teams. With excellent facilities and dedicated coaches, the mines and their subsidiaries provided players to most national teams.

For most Zambians, sport is soccer, with the others merely sideshows. Every school, village, and compound (shanty) town will have a team or teams. No need for boots at the grassroots level, and even the jerseys are unimportant—one side becoming "skins." With an *icimpombwa* (see page 98), the game is ready to start.

At the highest level, Zambia has a Super League and a Division One, with all teams professional or semi-professional and sponsored by companies or the Zambian Defence Force. The better players used to drift to South Africa for more pay and improved conditions, but that has all changed, with the top clubs able to attract quality Ugandan and Kenyan players.

With a FIFA ranking of 88 (2017), Zambia's national team is known as the Copper Bullets (Chipolopolo), and has a huge following throughout the country. Match day at the Levy Mwanawasa Stadium in Ndola is a mass of orange and green, dancing humanity blowing *vuvuzelas* (plastic horns). Those who can't get tickets cram into bars to watch the games on TV.

The nation suffered a massive loss in April 1993, when the entire soccer team, coaches, officials, a journalist, and crew were killed in a plane crash off the coast of Gabon on its way to Dakar to play a World Cup qualifier against Senegal. The country was in profound shock when, effectively, the golden age of Zambian soccer was wiped out. The team was coached by two former national legends, Alex Chola and Godfrey "Ucar" Chitalu, and was full of household names. But none can forget the sheer explosion of joy in 2012, when Zambia beat Côte d'Ivoire in Gabon to win the African Cup of Nations a few hundred meters from the crash site. Recent success for the junior Chipolopolo at the Under-20 Africa Cup of Nations came in the 2017 tournament, where the team beat Senegal 2–0 at the Heroes Stadium in Lusaka.

Boxing has always had a following in Zambia, and the nation has regularly picked up medals at the Commonwealth Games, as well as African and Commonwealth titles. Perhaps the most famous boxers of recent years have been Catherine Phiri, who won the WBC bantamweight title in Mexico in January 2016, and Esther Phiri, former WIBA and IBO junior welterweight champion.

Zambia has enormous potential in athletics, with children in the rural areas running long distances to school every day. At the same time, there is probably no finer ground for strengthening muscle groups than sand, which harks back to the 1970s and '80s, when students from the Western Province won all the interprovincial cross-country championships. Samuel Matete from Chingola has been Zambia's most successful athlete, claiming one Olympic silver medal and three World Championship silver medals.

Cricket was formerly the preserve of the Asian and expatriate communities, but great strides have been made to introduce the sport into schools and institutes of higher learning. The Midlands (Kabwe and Lusaka) and the Copperbelt are the main centers, with women's cricket beginning to make a breakthrough and national age-group teams being formed.

Golf courses are found in all the bigger towns, with a very pleasant nine-hole course at State House. There is also an interesting course at the Mkushi Country Club, where the "greens" are sand and must be smoothed with a scraper. The Zambia Sugar Open Golf Championship and the KCM Zambia Open Golf Championship are the premier events on the annual calendar, and attract golfers from all over the world as part of the Sunshine Tour. All the courses are open to tourists and business travelers.

Squash, badminton, volleyball, basketball, and table tennis have leagues and representative teams, with most associated with the Midlands and the Copperbelt. Polo has its followers, largely among the white residents of Lusaka and Mazabuka, and in the 2015 Polocrosse (a

hybrid sport mixing polo and lacrosse) World Cup,
Zambia finished runners-up to South Africa.

MUSIC AND DANCE

In Zambia music is life, and every opportunity is
taken to listen. There is the stereotypical Tonga man
who rides a bicycle gripping the handlebar with one
hand and holding a radio to his ear with the other.
There isn't a home without music—background
noise to the daily running of a family, perhaps,
but regardless of the genre it's there, coming from
a radio, a Hi-Fi system, or a speaker dock. Music
accompanies everything in Zambia, and is even sent
abroad—singers Samantha Mumba and Emeli Sande
have Zambian fathers.

Things have moved forward from the pure
percussive sounds heard in the villages (and
nowadays in the tourist dining rooms and cultural
centers) to the use of mixers, layering, and
synthesizers in recording studios. Most Zambians still
have a nostalgic love for the Zamrock and Kalindula
of the 1970s and '80s. Kalindula music and dance is
uniquely Zambian, coming originally from Luapula
Province; it uses a throbbing bass line, playing dead
notes or muffled strings against a tight percussion
background. Famous for providing the backdrop for
the grinding, gyrating dancing queens, Kalindula
saw the rise of the character dancers "Mr. Toilet" and
"Chosa" and the evergreen international stage act
"Amayenge."

Zed HipHop and ZedBeats have their own stars,
with lyrics that tend to reflect current political and
social issues and with twerking songstresses thrusting
hips while squatting low in unlikely locations.

Unsurprisingly, Gospel music is very popular, and new artists are trying to infuse bible texts into music with a rhumba beat or a hip-hop/R&B rhythm.

Music and dance are inseparable in Zambia, and every ethnic group has its own dances and songs that are featured on festive occasions. Each dance is subtly different, involving unique rhythms, steps, body, head, and shoulder movements. To the Westerner, the dances and music look and sound pretty much the same, but each is as individual as the language of the singing. In the village context, music and dance provide entertainment for the local people and an opportunity to socialize.

The music for the dance is mainly provided by drums of different sizes made from hollowed-out tree trunks and dried, cured goatskins. Rattles, shakers, and a variety of anklets are also used. The Ngumbo, Bisa, and Ushi people of Luapula Province use large empty oil drums, which are cut into halves and covered with dried, cured goatskins at both ends. These are laid horizontally, and arc hit with

mallet drumsticks by a drummer at each end. In performing the *akalela* dance, whistle blowing features prominently when the male and female dancers are static and gyrating. Using the side of the drum produces a harder, metallic note, and this accompanies the whistle blowing when the dancer is moving the hips in a stationary position. The *akalela* can be competitive, and teams vie for supremacy in terms of choreography and song lyrics, with teams from Luapula Province traveling to the Copperbelt. The *mgunda* dance of the Tumbuka from Eastern Province is performed by male dancers, and again it can have a competitive edge.

For the Tumbuka in the villages, the Vimbuza spiritual healing ritual involves singing and specific drum rhythms, which are used to enable the patients to take in the spirits. These spirits help the patients to overcome the problems they are facing by exorcizing their psychological maladies through dance. Today, however, the visitor is likely to see the Vimbuza spirit dance performed away from the villages, and removed from its original healing context, in community and cultural centers and hotels.

ARTS AND CRAFTS

Zambia has some astonishing artists, whose work may be viewed at galleries in Lusaka, the Copperbelt, or Livingstone. Most have been self-taught, overcoming the high cost of materials and the reluctance of many of the indigenous population to part with their hard-earned kwacha for wall decorations and ornaments. Their passion and creativity, using a variety of materials and techniques, are outstanding.

As well as the galleries, there are hotels, corporate business houses, embassies, game lodges, and museums that have a range of high-quality art, sometimes for sale. Look at the work of the watercolorist Peter Maibwe, the late sculptor and musician Flinto Chandia, Stary Mwaba, William Miko, the late Godfrey Setti, Laurence Yombwe, Agness Yombwe, the late Trevor (Brian) Ford of "Yuss" cartoon fame, Vic Guhrs, the late Henry Tayali, and the precocious Mwamba Chikwemba.

Masquerade masks used by the Makishi in the North-Western Province and the Nyau masks from the east are wonderfully made from local materials, including wood, animal hides, plant fibers, and feathers. These are usually on display, as are wooden masks and other crafted wooden objects at the specialist curio stores found in the Copperbelt, Lusaka, and Livingstone. Baskets made from natural fibers (roots from the *makenge* bushes and leaves from the *ilala* palm) by the

Lozi, Mbunda, and Tonga people are world renowned, and are readily available in curio stores and markets.

The Kabwata Cultural Centre, Northmead market, the Sunday market at the Arcades Mall, and the market at the Dutch Reformed Church held on the last Saturday every month, are all in Lusaka, and here you can find every conceivable traditional handmade craft—paintings; carvings in wood, soapstone, and malachite; bowls; jewelry; masks; *chitenge*; knitted hats; and so on. In the Copperbelt, the Obote Avenue market has arts-and-crafts stalls, and many artists and sculptors sell their wares along the Ndola-Kitwe Road. Livingstone, the tourism capital, has curio and souvenir outlets in the town center, including Mukuni Park, and while you are viewing the Victoria Falls you will hardly be able to avoid the vendors next to the Falls Museum. You must bargain, and be prepared to move to another stall if the price you are willing to pay is not accepted.

So what are the must-have items to choose from this hotbed of creativity? Perhaps some meters of high-quality *chitenge* material (Java wax print) from a trader in Freedom Way or Kabwata in Lusaka, some Kabwe silver jewelry, copper ornaments, and malachite pendants and necklaces. Hand-painted duvet covers, table mats, table runners, cushion covers, and animal wall hangings are easy to fold into a suitcase, and unframed artwork is light to carry and easily framed back home. Small wire cars are excellent gifts for children.

PLACES TO VISIT AND THINGS TO DO
• South or North Luangwa National Parks, for a walking safari
• Lake Kariba, one of the world's largest man-made lakes

- Victoria Falls, a World Heritage Site
- Livingstone Museum, for local artifacts and David Livingstone memorabilia
- Whitewater rafting, riverboarding, and kayaking, downstream of the Victoria Falls

- Microlight or helicopter flight over the Victoria Falls
- Livingstone, for a Sundowner Cruise on the Zambezi
- Bungee jumping or riding the bridge slide at the Victoria Falls Bridge
- Bangweulu Wetlands for birdwatching, especially the Shoebill Stork
- Kasanka National Park for the annual bat migration (October to December)
- Mongu, Western Province, for the Kuomboka Ceremony, when it is on
- Any venue for traditional dance and music
- Lusaka's Arcades Mall for the Sunday market
- Lusaka's Kalimba Reptile Park
- Copperbelt, for the Chimfunshi Wildlife Sanctuary and Chimpanzee Orphanage

chapter seven

TRAVEL, HEALTH, & SAFETY

Traveling in Zambia is always an adventure, with road and rail journeys providing the most excitement. For the motorist in the cities, the sheer volume of traffic, the lack of parking spaces, and the countless street hawkers ready to risk life and limb for a sale can produce many hair-pulling moments. For those using trunk roads, there are the potholes, the boredom of an endless bush vista, and the nagging concern of what to do in the event of a breakdown. For the rail user, keeping to the published timetable can be tricky. So much easier by plane!

ARRIVAL

Most people will arrive in Zambia through the international airports in Lusaka (Kenneth Kaunda), Livingstone (Harry Mwaanga Nkumbula), Ndola (Simon Mwansa Kapwepwe), and Mfuwe in the South Luangwa National Park. The Kenneth Kaunda Airport is currently undergoing a US $400 million upgrade, and is due for completion in 2019. The Harry Mwaanga Nkumbula Airport has been extensively modernized and refurbished.

By road, Zambia can be reached through Malawi (at the Mwami/Mchinji, the best and most efficient border post), through Tanzania (Tunduma/Nakonde), through the Democratic Republic of the Congo (Kasumbalesa, Mokambo, or Sakania border posts), through Zimbabwe (Livingstone, Chirundu, or Kariba Dam border posts), through Namibia (Katimo Mulilio Bridge), or through Botswana (Kasungula Ferry—a US \$253 million road/rail bridge is scheduled to be completed in 2019). There is a rail link, TAZARA (Tanzania–Zambia Railway), from Kapiri Mposhi in Zambia to Dar es Salaam in Tanzania. Stretching more than 1,160 miles (1,860 km), this early exhibition of Chinese technical expertise, and their beneficence in view of the closure of the southern route through Rhodesia (Zimbabwe) by the white government there, was officially opened in 1976.

A more extreme way of arriving in Zambia is via the Motor Vessel *Liemba*, taking the weekly sailing from Kigoma on Lake Tanganyika in western Tanzania to Mpulungu in northern Zambia. The journey should take about two days, but much depends upon the stopping schedule along the route and how efficient the small boats are that carry cargo and passengers to the vessel (only Kigoma, Kasanga, and Mpulungu have jetties). The *Liemba* is the oldest serving ferry in the world. Built in Germany in 1913 and named the *Graf von Goetzen*, it was equipped with a four-inch gun and worked on Lake Tanganyika in the First World War. It was later scuttled, then salvaged, and brought back into service in 1927.

Crossing the Border
Assuming that you require a visa (visitors from SADC and COMESA countries do not), coming into Zambia is relatively easy, especially since the introduction of the e-visa, which permits entry and travel within

Zambia. Basically what you receive is an approval letter that informs you that your application has been successful; immigration officers at ports of entry can verify this on their system, but it is worth taking a hard copy of the letter with you. Upon arrival, you present your passport, the visa approval letter if requested, and the US $50 single entry visa fee (double/multiple entry is US $80) for a thirty-day tourist visa. A visa can, of course, be obtained from any port of entry without the e-visa (it saves time and the hassle of filling forms in after the journey) or at a Zambian mission abroad. There are countries whose nationals require visas prior to travel to Zambia, and you should check if yours is included in the list.

The introduction of a two-country visa for those who wish to visit both Zambia and Zimbabwe is ideal, especially since it allows unlimited trips between the two countries. The KAZA visa is available at the Kenneth Kaunda Airport, the Harry Mwaanga Nkumbula Airport, the Victoria Falls land border, and the Kazungula land border with Botswana for those tourists who wish to visit Botswana for day trips through the Kasungula border. Again, this visa is available only to those nationals of countries who do not require visas prior to travel to Zambia. It costs US $50, and is also valid for thirty days, but it does not appear to be in an e-visa format at this point. Be warned that, whatever visa you decide to get, there will be long lines at the immigration desks.

On flying out of Zambia there is an airport tax (National Airports Corporation levy) that must be paid by all departing passengers on both international and domestic flights. This can be paid in US dollars or Zambian kwacha (US $30 for international flights and US $11 for domestic flights).

GETTING AROUND THE COUNTRY
By Air

The quickest way to get around is obviously by air (most flights are operated by Proflight Zambia), and for the business traveler the industrial heartland of the Copperbelt is accessible by direct flights from Lusaka to Ndola (Simon Kapwepwe Airport), as is the booming mining town of Solwezi and the coffee capital of Zambia, Kasama. For the tourist, flights to Livingstone, Mfuwe, the Lower Zambezi, and the Liuwa Plains are all from Lusaka. The same company operates flights to Lilongwe (Malawi) and Durban in South Africa.

By Rail

"Let the train take the strain," the old British Rail slogan pronounced, and there is no better way to see the Zambian countryside. Aside from the TAZARA line, running northeastward from the terminal at Kapiri Mposhi to Dar es Salaam with a twice weekly service, there is the Kitwe–Lusaka–Livingstone line operated by Zambia Railways. If you have time aplenty, this line allows you to see something of the scenery and life in the villages along the track. A passenger embarking in Lusaka on Friday can expect to be in Livingstone about thirteen hours later, using the Zambezi train, which has a range of seat classes, sleeper cars, and a snack car. The Kafue train, which departs from Lusaka on Mondays, offers only economy seating for the journey, which takes the same length of time to cover the 293 miles (471 km).

Intercity Buses

Your starting point is probably going to be the Intercity Bus Terminus in Lusaka. From here, everywhere in Zambia is within reach. Note that there is a ban on public service vehicles traveling between 9:00 p.m. and 5:00 a.m., due to the high accident rate at night. Substandard road markings and signage, poor standards of driving, vehicles broken down or moving without lights, whimsical nocturnal animals crossing roads at the wrong time, and badly engineered and constructed roads make driving at night difficult. Coach or bus travel in the daytime makes good sense, as it is cheap (about US $25 from Lusaka to Livingstone) and generally comfortable, with the better companies offering air-conditioning, food, on-board toilet facilities, and TV.

Expect to be bewildered initially by the general confusion of the place—the noise, the swirl of humanity, and the sheer amount of luggage that everyone seems to have. Suitcases, boxes, and life's treasures wrapped up in *chitenge* bundles are head-carried towards vehicles that are waiting to be filled before departure. If you are not sure where your coach or bus departs from, just check out the bus bays, ordered according to their destination. Be prepared to be harassed by rowdy call boys who will endeavor to get you onto "their" bus. Be prepared to be fought over like a valuable carcass—the bus owners pay the youths for each passenger they bring. Look after your bags, and be mindful of the old ploy of rogue passengers who occupy seats in the buses in order to make it appear that they are nearly full and ready to depart.

It takes roughly seven hours to reach Livingstone from Lusaka, so with a 6.30 a.m. start you could be at the Victoria Falls by 2:00 p.m.

AROUND TOWN

The cheapest way to get around in the towns is by minibus, and for the adventurous this is a fine way to see urban life. To the newcomer the minibus system might be regarded as the commute from hell, with undesignated stops, maniacal drivers, and conductors who can count quickly but have never heard of the word "civil." It's all about getting as many customers as possible, and here the call boys lend a hand, shouting out destinations and shepherding clients toward waiting buses. The driver takes off as soon and as fast as the sixteen-seater will allow. Standing time is dead time, and the object is to keep moving!

There are points to note if you are going to travel by minibus: at a bus station, look for one that looks roadworthy in order to avoid delays at one of the innumerable police road blocks; make sure you have adequate small change; and hold on tightly to your personal items. You might say that the minibuses are cheap and cheerful and, indeed, the general feeling inside is one of camaraderie, group stoicism—and wanting to get out!

A more effective way of getting about, if you want to avoid the mayhem of the minibuses, is to take a taxi. The cost from the Kenneth Kaunda Airport to town is approximately US $30. The large towns have plenty, and there are always lines near the main hotels and markets. Before setting off in a taxi it is important to agree on the cost, and it is advisable to get an approximate figure by asking at the place where you are staying. If you have several meetings to attend, or indeed places to visit, hiring a taxi for a day can make sense as long as it is agreed that payment is by the mile or by the hour, and ensure you make a note of the mileage or the time when you start off.

ROADS AND DRIVING

Driving in daylight in Zambia can be a pleasure, providing that you have a robust, well-maintained vehicle that is unlikely to break down or have a flat. Vehicles drive on the left, as in the UK. Roads that are unpleasant to drive on are the Lusaka to Copperbelt interprovincial road passing through Kabwe and

Kapiri Mposhi, the Ndola–Kitwe–Chingola road, and the Chingola–Solwezi road (a new road is due to be constructed), because of the large volume of traffic. Much of

the traffic is heavy goods vehicles shuttling between the industrial or mining heartland of the Copperbelt and Lusaka, and the poor state of the roads does not  help. The Kasumbalesa–Chililabombwe–Chingola road, also in the Copperbelt, has to take the strain of the heavy goods vehicles plying their trade between the Democratic Republic of the Congo and Zambia. The Great East Road to Chipata in the Eastern Province has tortuous bends and big vehicles going to and coming from Malawi.

There are, however, some positives for daytime driving in Zambia. The traffic on the highways, aside from the Livingstone to the Copperbelt roads, is relatively light, and you have the road to yourself for miles. You cross the Kafue River and pass through a national park on the way to Mongu. Stop in the middle of nowhere, and there's silence, apart from the sound of ringnecked doves and helmeted guineafowl—the sounds of Africa.

Make sure that you have plenty of water, food, and fuel on board; that everyone is wearing seat belts; and that the vehicle registration documents, two metallic emergency triangles (with two white reflective stickers on the front and red reflective stickers on the back), and your driver's license, passport, and proof of insurance are all to hand.

At road blocks, slow down gently, turn off your music, and give the officer a cheery greeting— cigarettes on the dashboard used to be a welcome ice-breaker. If stopped by traffic police for a recognizable offense, such as speeding (the limit on main roads is 60 mph / 100 kmh), be polite and friendly. If you are required to pay a fine there and then, you should be issued with a ticket that details the offense, together with a receipt.

To pay at the tollgates that are springing up on all the major roads out of the towns, be ready with your cash, at least until a digitized payment system is in place. The revenues from the tollgates, together with the levying of heavy goods vehicles at points of entry into the country and truck scales, are expected to make the maintenance of these roads self-financing.

Potholes are a part of life for anyone on the roads in Zambia, and are to be avoided. In a pothole, your vehicle's tires sink to the crushed hardcore below the road surface; tires, rims, and suspension suffer on impact with the hard edges of the hole; and the hole enlarges. Associated with the rainy season and the tendency by maintenance contractors to use the bare minimum of asphalt, these monsters lurk ready to snare the unwary night driver and the speedster.

WHERE TO STAY

Lusaka is the main business hub, and it offers a range of accommodation types, from internationally recognized top-end hotels such at the Radisson Blu, the Taj Pamodzi, the InterContinental, and the Southern Sun Ridgeway, through a selection of mid-range groups including Protea, Cresta, and Best Western. There are many smaller private lodges—these are often converted homes—and hotels in the capital, and two large lodges with private nature reserves forty minutes away.

In the Copperbelt there are some long-established hotels, lodges, and guesthouses as well as newer ones in Kitwe, Ndola, and Chingola. For business visitors going further afield to the mines of North-Western Province, there are a couple of superb hotels in Solwezi.

Livingstone has an impressive choice of accommodation to suit all tastes and budgets. At the top end are the hotels situated by the Victoria Falls and the Zambezi River, where, in addition to luxury accommodation and service, you are paying handsomely for the privilege of hearing and seeing "the smoke that thunders." Along the banks of the Zambezi, going upriver through the Mosi-oa-Tunya National Park, are some extraordinary secluded and sumptuous lodges, thatched chalets, and tented accommodation, with amazing river views, all with game drives, fishing, and cruises. Downstream, the Zambezi can be viewed as it meanders eastward through the Batoka Gorge.

Nearer the town center accommodation prices fall, and there are some excellent places to stay including hotels (the predictable Protea, a well-known African brand of Marriott International, is here), lodges, and a backpackers' hostel.

Zambia has twenty National Parks, with nine fully developed for tourism; importantly, most are accessible all year round. All the Parks charge an entry fee and a conservation and community levy, which help to maintain anti-poaching levels and provide for the welfare of the local people. In the valley of the Luangwa River, the South Luangwa National Park is considered by many to be the finest game park in Africa, with stunning accommodation in the form of lodges and tented bush games set within one of the world's greatest wildlife sanctuaries. Walking safaris were pioneered here, and the park is served by the international airport at Mfuwe. The North Luangwa National Park has two small, established camps, and is open for only four months of the year, with most visitors arriving by air from Mfuwe. Here all the game viewing is on foot, where getting close to nature takes on a new meaning.

To combine longer game viewing, birdwatching, and fishing, the visitor will need to go to the Lower Zambezi National Park, where the Zambezi River flows along its southern edge, or the Kafue National

Park. Here there is a choice of land and water safaris and a range of lodges, tented accommodation, and self-catering chalets. There are airstrips at Royal and Jeki for the Lower Zambezi National Park and at Ngoma, Chunga, Hippo, and the Busanga Plains in the Kafue National Park.

For something a little different, the visitor might try a visit to the Bangweulu Wetlands and stay in the Shoebill Island Camp after a journey by 4x4 and banana boat, or by private charter plane to the airstrip near the

camp. The visitor will be accommodated in well-appointed meru-style tents (large, rectangular tents, with an opening at the front and a covered veranda) with panoramic views over the wetlands; there is a campsite as well for those who wish for something more robust. There are banana boat trips into the depths of the swamps, game viewing (there are a vast number of the rare black lechwe), and birdwatching, including trekking to see the remarkable shoebill stork. A stay on Shoebill Island combines well with a visit to Kasanka National Park to see the largest migration of mammals in the world, as millions of straw-colored fruit bats descend to the swamp forest to eat after migrating from the DRC.

If time allows, the visitor should seize the opportunity to visit the extraordinary Shiwa Ngandu Estates, north of Mpika, in Muchinga Province. On land purchased in 1914, Sir Stewart Gore Brown succeeded in creating a vast English country estate, which, after much refurbishment, remains in family ownership. It is open to guests, who can enjoy walks, drives, and horse safaris to watch game and birds. Accommodation on the estate is within the manor house, the splendid Impandala farmhouse nearby, or at the Kapishya Hot Springs Lodge. Bearing in mind that there are 460 miles (740 km) between Lusaka and Shiwa Ngandu, many visitors prefer to take a charter flight from Lusaka, Mfuwe, or Ndola to the landing strip on the estate.

HEALTH

For the ordinary Zambian, being ill is fraught with many problems. Not least is how to access treatment. There is a three-level system with free health care for Zambians: a stay in the hospital will require the patient to decide whether to opt to use the more basic facilities or pay for an upgrade to what is called "High Cost." Wealthy Zambians will invariably seek treatment in South Africa or India.

Health insurance is essential for visitors, and must cover evacuation and treatment in case of an accident or sudden illness. Generally, medical facilities in the private sector are good, but they are poor in the district hospitals and clinics in rural areas, and it is advisable to know your blood type and carry a sterile medical kit that includes needles, dressings, and so on. Regardless of insurance, you should have access to sufficient funds to pay up-front medical expenses.

It is a good idea to have a medical check-up four to six weeks before arrival in Zambia, and to ensure that the necessary vaccinations for typhoid, tetanus, and Hepatitis A are completed. There is a low potential for exposure to yellow fever in parts of Zambia, and vaccination is generally not recommended. Travelers arriving from countries with risk of yellow fever transmission, and those having traveled for more than twelve hours through an airport of such a country, should have a certificate of yellow fever vaccination.

Malaria occurs widely in Zambia, and the mosquitoes that cause it are more active in the hot, rainy season, when there is plenty of surface water for breeding purposes. Visitors should start a course of antimalarial prophylaxis prior to departure and sleep under treated mosquito nets. Using insect repellents (DEET-based) is recommended for use before evening activities, and plug-in insecticides help in the bedroom.

In 2015, around 55,000 adults became infected with HIV in Zambia, largely as a result of unprotected heterosexual sex. The advice for visitors is to abstain from sex with anyone whose HIV status is unknown. Appropriate precautions should be taken if engaging in activities that may run the risk of HIV infection and STDs. Heightened sexual risktaking abroad is often linked to increased alcohol intake, and with the large number of bars and clubs and the proliferation of sex workers, the visitor needs to be aware of this.

Any opportunity to dip toes into the Zambezi should be offset by thoughts of bilharzia and schistosomiasis. Schistosoma larvae are released from infected snails that can penetrate human skin following contact and migrate to body organs. As a rule of thumb, if the water is moving rapidly (whitewater rafters take note), there is nothing to worry about, but to avoid the risk of a rash, itchy skin, fever, chills, and the possibility of an intestinal or bladder infection, it is best to avoid rivers and lakes.

SAFETY

Visitors to Zambia want to take the opportunities that abound, and appreciate the color, noise, and vibrancy alongside the scenery and wildlife. They like to join in, and immerse themselves in the African scene—which unfortunately includes a criminal element that seeks to exploit the newcomer. Serious crime includes armed robberies, residential break-ins, vehicle hijacking, and sexual assaults, with security issues becoming manifestly more challenging after dark.

When driving, it is not advisable to stop for hitchhikers. Also, be on the lookout for objects that have been placed across the road. If you see any, approach very warily, and be ready to reverse.

Care must be taken when approaching locked gates at night, as carjackers may park behind their victim's vehicle, preventing it from reversing, and make an assault while the car waits to pass through security.

In public places, pickpocketing, bag snatching, distraction theft, and stealing from parked vehicles are common in high pedestrian areas such as markets, shopping areas, bus and railway stations, and tourist hotspots such as at the Victoria Falls. Valuable documents and passports should be kept in a hotel or lodge safe. Carry copies with you.

Being discreet and unostentatious helps to avoid trouble: phones, cameras, jewelry, and large amounts of money are best kept out of sight. If you have a vehicle, paid parking areas are found in Livingstone, Lusaka, and the bigger towns, and are the safest places for your car and its contents.

chapter eight

BUSINESS BRIEFING

THE BUSINESS ENVIRONMENT

Zambia has much to offer the overseas investor. First and foremost, it has political stability, with a working, multiparty democracy and legal, banking, and insurance systems that are comparable to Western standards. Situated within the eastern, central, and southern African sphere of influence, and sharing a border with nine countries, it is well positioned as a regional hub for trade and communications, and the fact that Zambians are comfortable with the English language is an added bonus.

Zambia is ranked at 98 in the World Bank Report "Ease of Doing Business" (2017), with countries ranked from 1 (New Zealand) to 190 (Somalia), and occupies eighth position within Africa's fifty-four countries. It has an attractive portfolio of investment incentives, it is well placed to attract foreign capital, and with a GDP annual growth rate of 3.6 percent (2015)—down from 7.1 percent (2014) largely as a result of the copper market—Zambia has enormous resources. There are vast mineral reserves; 162,162 square miles (42 million sq. km.) of the land is suitable for arable farming, with only 5791 square miles (1.5 million sq. km.) used each year; and the twenty national parks and thirty-four game

management areas cover 25,097 square miles (6.5 million sq. km.).

Direct foreign investment is vital if Zambia is to increase employment and growth and improve the tax base and tax revenue. The government is keen to promote or develop agriculture, mining, tourism, energy, infrastructure, and manufacturing. Each sector has specific priorities for development, and all areas are liable for fiscal and non-fiscal incentives upon an undertaking to invest not less than US $500,000. Tax incentives affecting income tax and VAT with specific benefits for investment in agriculture, manufacturing, tourism, and mining are generous, and there are customs duty incentives with a duty refund scheme when specific conditions are met. Also beneficial is the fact that Zambia has signed Double Taxation Agreements with a number of countries, including the UK. An investor who puts US $250,000 or more into any sector is entitled to an Investor's Permit/License with certain non-fiscal benefits.

The Zambia Development Agency (ZDA) is responsible for marketing and promoting Zambia as the best investment destination. It provides comprehensive details of the business opportunities, incentives, and requirements for each sector, and further information on labor and land considerations.

In Zambia there are two categories of land: state land, which comprises 6 percent of the land and is used by district councils for residential, commercial, and industrial use; and customary land, which comprises 94 percent of the land and is controlled by traditional chiefs (women are not allowed to inherit this land). Without a freehold system, land is leased for ninety-nine years, renewable for a further ninety-nine years. Customary land can be converted to leasehold, which allows the lessee to use it as collateral. For the non-Zambian investor, there is the opportunity to acquire land assuming that the ordinances for recognition as an entrepreneur are in place and that the rather lengthy proceedings to fulfill the conditions for leasing are followed.

For some investors it is easier to acquire plots on land designated for manufacturing and farming. There are six Multi-Facility Economic Zones (MFEZ) / Industrial Parks where the government is providing hard and soft infrastructure to support the private sector in both manufacturing-related industries and those related to the export trade. Within the farm blocks, local and foreign investors have ready access to surveyed land for agricultural production as well as basic infrastructure and community support.

There is no doubt that, while the investment opportunities in Zambia appear good, the overseas

investor needs to be patient. The paper trail of
registration, permits, and licenses seems endless,
and ultimately increases the transaction costs for the
investors. The One Stop Shop designed to provide
the local and foreign investor with quick and efficient
registration services has not been able to mobilize the
different agencies effectively, and, at the same time,
power outages have affected investor confidence.

BUSINESS CULTURE

The buying and selling of goods, including food
items, has sustained vast numbers of the population
for many years, with street vendors a part of the
urban and rural landscape. Making a profit from
small-scale retailing provides many families with
basic needs, with the women often in charge. As
well as the marketeers, there are myriad small and
medium-sized enterprises engaged in manufacturing,
trading industrial products and agricultural inputs,
printing, services, and small-scale mining and
quarrying.

If you can't find work in the formal job market, the obvious path is to become self-employed, and Zambians are eager to do so. There is a whole host of associations and unions that oversee the running of various sectors, from the Marketeers Association of Zambia to the Zambia Bus and Taxi Workers Union. For the needy entrepreneur there are microfinance institutions and a range of government initiatives, such as the Stella Project in Lusaka and the Presidential Empowerment Initiative to help marketeers across the country; this particular initiative has seen market traders in the Copperbelt refuse to pay back 1.3 million ZMW given out in soft loans.

There are trade associations for specific industries with the Zambia Chamber of Commerce and Industry (ZACCI), representing several thousand businesses with corporate members, academia members, chamber members, and association members spread throughout the country and a dedicated secretariat in Lusaka. Providing advice and training, the ZACCI is a perfect avenue for networking with various functions, including breakfast meetings, gala dinners, and of course sponsored golf tournaments.

Representing a significant number of large and small-scale manufacturing enterprises, The Zambia Association of Manufacturers (ZAM) also has a secretariat and is geared toward promoting the interests of industrialists and manufacturers in Zambia. Membership of ZACCI and ZAM is important for all incomers pursuing business interests in Zambia, as it allows friendships to develop and new commercial avenues to open. Joining a service club, such as the Lions or the Rotary, is a good way not only to meet people but, at the same time, to understand and contribute to the local community.

THE ROLE OF NGOS

There are a large number of NGOs and civil society organizations in Zambia that provide services and assist the government. Their involvement stretches from the sourcing and provision of water to rural communities to the provision of legal aid to the vulnerable. Local NGOs are prominent in gender-based issues, particularly gender-based violence, inheritance, and women's rights in general. Many of these are affiliated to the Non-Governmental Organizations' Co-ordinating Council (NGOCC), which has seen tremendous work in empowering people, especially women and children. Local and international NGOs have over the years sought to address HIV/AIDs issues including counseling, training, and positive-status stigmatization. All the big non-business, non-state, not-for-profit organizations, such as Amnesty International, Oxfam International, and Doctors without Borders, operate in Zambia.

With more than four hundred NGOs registered with the government, they provide an immediate source of advice and assistance for the expatriate. Of course there is the dichotomy that while the NGOs are addressing issues of poverty, disease, gender equality and equity, and basic civil rights, the expatriates, including many aid and NGO workers, are enjoying the fruits of corporate and foreign country altruism with large 4x4 vehicles, subsidized housing, and foreign exchange salaries.

PERSONNEL

Once the investor has been granted an Investor's Permit, an application for a residency or self-employment permit can be made and applications for the employment of foreign workers formalized. For companies investing more than US $250,000 and employing more than two hundred workers, five expatriate employees may be brought in who may work for two years in the country. Expatriates are not permitted to take Human Resource positions. During their two-year work period, these expatriates are required to train Zambian understudies, who will take the positions when the permit expires.

There is a pool of talent in Zambia with high schools, colleges, technical and vocational institutions, and universities producing large numbers of graduates who enter the job market every year. With twenty-two universities alone, with Schools of Education, Health Science, Social Sciences, Business and Management, Medicine, Law, Media and Fine Arts, Science and Technology, Veterinary Medicine, Engineering, Environment and Tourism, and Mines and Agricultural Sciences, Zambia is well placed to provide skilled staff in most positions. In addition, the Zambia Institute of Chartered Accountants (ZICA) has accountancy and taxation programs, and

the Zambia Centre for Accountancy Studies (ZCAS) offers undergraduate and postgraduate degrees and a range of professional studies including Chartered Institute of Management Accounts (CIMA) and Association of Chartered Certified Accountants (ACCA).

The investor should have no problem finding skilled and unskilled staff locally, and here the government has been taken to task regarding the high number of expatriate workers in the country. Citing cases of foreign workers employed in middle management positions and Chinese laborers working on the roads, the government has not managed to carry out a meaningful program of "Zambianization"—a buzz word since the 1970s.

Whether local or foreign labor is used, the Department of Labour under the Ministry of Labour and Social Security is responsible for labor policy, while the Zambia Federation of Employers communicates the position of employers. Working conditions, including the minimum wage, are closely regulated, and it is expected that wages or salaries include allowances for housing, transportation, children's medical and educational expenses, utility bills, and holiday travel for senior staff. Non-cash benefits may include subsidized canteens, sporting facilities, and transport to and from work.

Office hours are normally 8:00 a.m. to 5:00 p.m. Monday to Friday and 8:00 a.m. to 1:00 p.m. on Saturdays, or to 5:00 p.m. in the case of retail businesses. Under the Minimum Wages and Conditions of Employment Act, the normal weekly hours should not exceed forty-eight; employees working after 5:00 p.m. are to be paid time and a half, and double time on Sundays and public holidays.

Annual paid leave of no fewer than twenty-four days should be given, and an employee is entitled to seven days' paid leave on the death of a spouse, child, or parent. In the event of the death of an employee, a spouse, registered children, or other dependants, the employer must provide a coffin, cash, and maize meal for the wake. For the employer, the advent of AIDS can severely impact upon business, with many man-days lost as families mourn the passing of loved ones, together with the financial consequences implied in funeral grants and reduced worker productivity.

MEETINGS

Business meetings are seen as a critical step in forming and later cementing relationships and are taken seriously, with due formality and the observance of procedure.

The meeting carries more weight if it is prearranged in a formal letter or e-mail and has an agenda that can be loosely followed. Confirm it shortly beforehand with a friendly follow-up. Investors may have to be patient with government ministries and the multitude of agencies that need to be reached despite the One Stop Shop, and telephone calls may be necessary—it is always useful to have the name and if possible the cell phone number of the person you want to meet.

Meeting times should be strictly adhered to, even though the government official may be tardy; it is his or her prerogative to be late, and it implies a busy schedule. It is important to be smartly dressed, preferably in a suit or jacket and tie.

Business cards provide a personal touch, and are very important. Nothing beats a person-to-person meeting sealed with a firm handshake and an exchange of business cards. Also there are always opportunities in Zambia to make valuable business connections—at a function, trade show, airport lounge, or golf club, and a business card can make a memorable first impression, particularly if it is creative and looks different—your Zambian contact probably has hundreds of standard cards.

Meetings in Zambia can be lengthy affairs, with everyone entitled to a say and with much deliberation over each point. Seating is prescribed if large numbers are involved, with the minister or CEO at the head of the table. Prior to his or her arrival, it is typical for people to shake hands and engage in friendly small talk, then to stand when he or she enters. People are expected to introduce themselves formally at the start of the meeting, and it is important that eye contact is made in the introduction. At the end of the meeting there is always an opportunity for networking.

PRESENTATIONS

For the investor, this is an opportunity to shine. A PowerPoint presentation will allow you to dictate the proceedings and lead the meeting to the conclusion that you require. Don't include too much text on each slide; a few words and some spontaneous talk are more engaging and natural. Include a brief summary of the key points of your presentation, and slip in your company logo whenever you can. Zambians quite rightly like data, and want you to prove the efficacy of your company or the project statistically and to recount previous successes to build credibility.

BUSINESS DIPLOMACY

The ability to negotiate is key for all who intend to invest in the country, whether it involves contracts, employment discussions, real estate leasing, labor and management talks, or handling disputes.

Zambians like to see that appropriate preparations have been made and that the problem has been properly analyzed. A friendly, non-adversarial approach is preferred, and much more can be achieved if formality is dispensed with. Zambians are not naturally confrontational, and will look for ways to find the commonalities for both sides so that matters can move forward and an agreement can be reached. Once this happens, it is important that both sides are clear about what has been decided and the course of action to be pursued to effect the decision.

For many in Zambia the way to move in business is by surfing on the backs of people you know—relations, old school chums, and friends. In any situation, once a link has been made matters can proceed expeditiously and business life can be more fruitful.

CONTRACTS AND LEGAL CONSIDERATIONS

Contracts are binding. Those involving land leasing, selling, purchasing, or renting need to be drawn up in conjunction with a reputable law firm. Any default may mean litigation and a court hearing.

The High Court can hear a civil claim exceeding a certain amount and has appellate jurisdiction from the Subordinate Court, which deals with claims up to a certain sum of money and the nature of the relief being sought by a party to a lawsuit. The Small Claims Courts determine lesser disputes, and self-representation is allowed. Specialist courts such as the

Industrial and Labour Relations Court and the Land Tribunal have the same judicial seniority as the High Court.

In the World Bank Report "Ease of Doing Business" (2017) Zambia ranks 135th out of 190 countries in the "Enforcing Contracts" table, which measures the cost and time taken for resolving a commercial dispute and the quality of the judicial processes.

TENDERS
The tendering system in Zambia is well developed, with UN agencies, embassies, and private companies advertising for bids. Government ministries and agencies are legally bound to put out tenders or bids for services, construction work, or the procurement of certain items or vehicles and the disposal of obsolete ones. Open or public tenders are advertised online, in newspapers, and in the Government Gazette through the Zambia Tender Board and overseen by the Zambia Public Procurement Authority for government contracts. The tenders are open to all, including foreign suppliers, and a time frame of six weeks from the date of publication is usually allowed.

There have been reports of fraud in the tendering process for government bids occurring during vendor selection, contracting, and maintenance. Facilitation payments to secure government contracts have been made and poor internal control systems have led to claims of corruption.

A LEVEL PLAYING FIELD
Women's representation in parliament is currently at 17 percent, and at the local government level at

9 percent, far below the African Union and SADC parity level of 50 percent at all levels. Having said that, women hold many key government positions.

The modern urban Zambian woman has made enormous strides in terms of education and in the workplace, and this is reflected in her aspirational lifestyle. Women now hold many middle-management positions, and the market vendor has moved into tech-savvy entrepreneurship. Little Miss Meek from the village has morphed into a cultured, sassy individual who wants to make things happen.

While women hold important posts in many organizations, commercial banks, and permanent missions abroad, including the United Nations, it is clear that more needs to be done to bring about greater equality. Here, the Gender Equity and Equality Act of 2015 is intended to narrow the gender gaps in the country. The proportion of female workers in the private sector has increased to more than 38 percent, higher than the average across all countries (34 percent). Access to microfinances has seen a growth of female entrepreneurs, and training programs have assisted in providing the guidelines for startups.

The role of women in business has been highlighted recently with the introduction of menstrual leave: all women in Zambia are allowed by law to take a day off each month (discreetly called "Mother's Day").

GIFT GIVING
Within a Zambian business environment, giving a gift can enhance a company's image and create a good impression, showing that you are pleased

to honor the recipient. However, it's always best to present only a small token, to avoid the gift being misconstrued as a bribe. A carefully wrapped, good-quality pen-and-pencil set, displaying a discreet company logo, perhaps with a business card inside with a personal handwritten note on the back, would be very acceptable. Gifts can be presented at the first meeting, and another token given at the conclusion of a contract. Always give, and indeed receive, with two hands in Zambia.

CORRUPTION

Corruption exists in Zambia at all levels, from the traffic police to high-level government technocrats. The government is aware of this, and has put in place measures to eliminate it. Transparency International's 2016 Corruption Perceptions Index placed Zambia in eighty-seventh place out of 187 countries (December 2016); a fall from seventy-sixth in 2015. The Index shows how corrupt the public sector is perceived to be, and for countries intent upon bringing in investment it is imperative that the taint of dishonesty be minimized.

The World Bank Enterprises Survey 2013 showed a positive trend in the control of corruption in Zambia; however, the same survey highlighted corruption as the second-most problematic factor for doing business (after access to finance) for the companies interviewed within the survey. Sixteen percent of companies in Zambia had experienced at least one payment request across six transactions dealing with taxes, licenses, permits, and access to utilities, with firms in Lusaka being exposed to corruption three times more than those elsewhere in the country.

Corruption and a weak institutional framework have hindered the business community, with bribery rampant in business operations. At the same time, foreign investors' property rights have not been adequately protected, with Zambia's land administration cited as being one of the most corrupt administrations in the country. Having said this, Zambia ranks thirteenth in Africa on the Corruption Perceptions Index, and matters are improving through legislation (the Public Disclosure Act provides legal protection for civil servants or public sector employees reporting cases of corruption) and the ratifying of various conventions, including the United Nations Convention Against Corruption and the African Union on Preventing and Combating Corruption.

There have been instances of grand corruption involving embezzlement and abuse of power by high-ranking officials including, more recently, the misuse of funds (US $3.4 million) given to the

Zambia National Farmers Union by Finland and Sweden. Some sectors stand out as being particularly corrupt. The Zambia Police Road Section has become notorious for extorting bribes at roadblocks, while the Prison Service has a deplorable record for brutality, corruption, the use of force, and the abuse of prisoners. A 2014 report showed that in eight out of ten interactions with the police, corruption had taken place.

For the businessperson, dealings with the Zambia Revenue Authority have been fraught with expectations to pay bribes in meetings with tax officials. However, the introduction of electronic systems has helped to minimize these by eliminating human interaction in the transaction processes. The Prohibition and Prevention of Money Laundering Act criminalizes money laundering, increases penalties for financial crimes, and now requires financial institutions to report suspicious transactions.

The Anti-Corruption Commission is charged with the fight against corruption in Zambia, and by October 2016 had 588 cases under investigation. At the same time, the Drug Enforcement Commission through its Anti-Money Laundering Unit has been successful in arresting a number of public figures. However, with a low conviction rate, public confidence has been severely undermined and the role of civil society organizations such as Transparency International has become increasingly important in monitoring corruption.

chapter nine

COMMUNICATING

LANGUAGE

The official language of Zambia is English, which is used in education and business. The World Linguistic Society put Zambia in second place in the list of the best English-speaking countries in Africa (2015). Most Zambians also speak their own local language plus one other, and can move fluidly from one language to another within the same conversation. The people of the Copperbelt largely speak English and Bemba, while those in Lusaka speak English and Nyanja. Intriguingly, the vernacular language of the Copperbelt is Lamba, with Bemba arriving in the early twentieth century with the migrants from Luapula, Northern, and Muchinga Provinces working in the copper mines. While the Bemba-speaking people moved to the Copperbelt, others whose lingua franca was Nyanja made their way from eastern Zambia to look for work in the new capital of Lusaka.

Zambians in Lusaka and the Copperbelt cities can distinguish between their own town's Bemba or Nyanja and that spoken in the rural heartlands of Northern and Eastern Provinces. It is quite possible for a Bemba-speaking person to travel to Isoka in Muchinga Province to visit grandparents and be unable to understand much of what is being said. The "deep" Bemba or Nyanja spoken in the villages has not been altered or merged with other languages, and newer "town" words or phrases have not been assimilated into everyday village life.

Languages are dynamic, changing with time, absorbing the new and forgetting the old. Zambians readily take borrowed words on board and slip them into their mother tongues. Without a word for a motorbike, all two-wheeled vehicles with an engine have become *hondas*, all toothpaste is *colgate*, and all types of floor polish *cobra*, after the South African wax brand. All cordials are *mazoe*, from the Zimbabwean orange crush, cooking oil is *saladi*, after the early Lever Brothers product, and any washing powder is *surf*, from the Unilever brand.

Two Zambians talking to each other in the vernacular may use both English and local words (in this case Bemba) that are based on English, for example: *shikafu* (scarf), *buku* (book), *belu* (bell), *gofu* (golf), and *kwini* (queen). The letter "r" does not appear in the Bemba language and they use the "l" instead. This can cause confusion—as in the pastor's homily about the need to "play," or the farmer's statement that he "bleeds pigs."

Zambians are past masters at providing new words and sayings for the everyday. Originating in the tough compounds, the new vocabulary spreads throughout the provinces and quickly becomes street talk. *Nshima* becomes *ka pulp*; a toilet is *shanks* (from the Armitage Shanks bathroom range); a person who gets drunk quickly is *one piston* (lacking strength); *michopo* is any form of grilled meat; something good is *laliga* (the Spanish premier soccer league); a street seller or unemployed person is *kaponya* (from the Bemba *ukuponya*, meaning "something dropped"); drunk becomes *belegede* (from the disabling disease that renders one paralysed and helpless); peanuts, called groundnuts in Zambia, are *gunpowder* (packed with protein and known to increase the male libido); and *kopala* is a streetwise boy or girl (from someone from the Copperbelt).

BODY LANGUAGE

Eye contact is a subtle form of interaction, and Zambians will use their eyes as much as their hands in a gesture or to signal comprehension. A young person should not look an elder in the eyes as this is disrespectful, and if a woman looks a man in the eye, this may be construed as flirting. Eye contact between equals of the same sex poses no problem and shows strength of character.

HUMOR

Zambians have an excellent sense of humor, and will laugh with abandon at a good stand-up comedian. Satire is much appreciated, and a Zambian is able to laugh at his or her own idiosyncrasies and affectations, even more so when the comedian is able to present an alter ego, as is the case with Bob Nkosha's "Dorika Ndaifulila."

Comedians may also poke fun at stereotypes of other ethnic groups, in the way that some English-speakers might joke about a Scotsman's thriftiness or a Texan's love of meat. The Bemba/Ngoni and the Tonga/Lozi "cousinship" lend themselves readily to such lampooning.

THE MEDIA

Zambians love news, and are politically astute when it comes to local and government affairs. The machinations of a relatively new political landscape provide good copy for a country with a small population and a short history. The interparty wrangling, the shuffling of the ministerial pack, the whiff of corruption, and prominent court cases make for essential viewing, listening, and reading—largely available through the private media. After all, as William Randolph Hearst, the American media magnate, once said, "News is something somebody doesn't want printed; all else is advertising."

The 2016 World Press Freedom Index ranked Zambia 114th out of 180 countries. In that year eighty-eight radio stations and nineteen television stations were operational. The low ranking reflects difficult times for the media, with the suspension by the Independent Broadcasting Authority of two radio stations (one subsequently had the ban lifted); the revocation of a TV license to broadcast (later reinstated); and the closure, and later liquidation, of an important investigative newspaper. The issue of an arrest warrant for the proprietor of *The Post* newspaper and the arrest of his wife further inflamed the situation.

The Media Institute of Southern Africa has soundly condemned what it sees as an attempt to silence criticism of the government and the harassment of journalists who seek to provide a voice to the opposition. The International Press Institute, the Committee to Protect Journalists, and rather bizarrely the National Union of Metalworkers of South Africa (NUMSA) have all registered their dismay at what they see as interference in the media by the government. The US-based Freedom House provided a "partly free"

rating for 2017 due to the restrictive environment for
the opposition in 2016 during the runup to the general
elections and the unequal media access.

The Press

The state-owned *Zambia Daily Mail* and *Times of
Zambia* have nationwide coverage, their views largely
reflecting the government's standpoint. With the
demise of *The Post*, which had been at the forefront of
breaking news and pursuing corruption since the early
1990s, the *Daily Nation* and *New Vision* (Lusaka) are
the only privately owned papers. The Internet news
media Web sites have had a significant role to play in
the dissemination of news alongside social platforms
such as Facebook and WhatsApp. The *Lusaka Times*,
Zambian Eye, *Lusaka Voice*, *Zambia Reports*, and
others provide online coverage of events in Zambia,
with some showing signs of distinct political bias.

TV and Radio

The Zambia National Broadcasting Corporation
(ZNBC) currently operates two television channels:
TV1 and TV 2—the latter being very much an

entertainment and business channel. In addition, the company operates four radio stations. Radio 1 broadcasts in one of the seven major local languages; Radio 2, Parliament Radio, and Radio 4 all broadcast in English.

Licensed TV stations have grown in number, and the wealthier people in the cities have access to a range of satellite-delivered pay TV services. South-Africa-based sports channels are popular for their soccer coverage, and the Nollywood soaps provide background comfort.

Radio use is widespread. Radio is particularly vital to the people in rural Zambia, providing news and light entertainment, together with religious, sporting, and educational content. The radio stations may be commercial, religious, or community, the last benefiting enormously from their ability to focus on local matters, providing a platform for the marginalized to connect with decision makers in the vernacular. Almost all districts now have community radio stations that may offer a different landscape from that espoused by the Public Service Broadcaster. Evelyn Hone College and the University of Zambia both have educational stations.

TELEPHONE AND INTERNET

Almost everyone in Zambia has a cell phone, or access to one (there are more than 12 million subscribers), and most have a prepaid plan that can be increased by purchasing prepaid cards for additional minutes. From the most rudimentary Nokia or Huawei to the iPhone 7 plus and Samsung S7 Edge, cell phones are readily available, with a choice of four mobile network providers; MTN has the largest number of subscribers.

A visitor would do well to purchase a cheap phone, buy a SIM card in Zambia, which must be registered at the time of purchase (the retailer will take a copy of your passport or work permit), and buy "Talk Time." For rural Zambians, the problem is finding a network and a way to charge the phone. Enterprising Zambian solar companies now market home systems with a 15- and 50-watt capacity—enough to charge a cell phone, switch on a light bulb, and power a small fan. Might there be business opportunities here?

Many Zambians are registered for Mobile Money, which allows them to use their cell phones for spending and bill payments, purchasing Talk Time, and transferring money. In rural Zambia, cell phones and text messaging are being used to speed up the time taken to deliver laboratory test results for HIV-exposed infants to the rural clinic and on to the mother. This method of contacting the mothers by health care workers enables the child to receive treatment and care earlier. A similar intervention has been applied to the early treatment of malaria.

Landlines are rarely found in homes in Zambia, partly because they lack the immediacy of the cell phone network and partly because of the difficulty of connection and repair by the state-owned Zamtel. Landlines have area codes, used only if the call is being made from outside the area.

There are more than five million mobile Internet users (2016) in Zambia, and with increasing smartphone usage this figure is growing. Fixed Internet subscriptions are a meager 35,000. 3G mobile has been introduced, and commercial 4G Long Term Evolution (LTE) is available, prompting an increase in mobile broadband subscribers. Some Internet Service Providers (ISPs) are using WiMAX wireless broadband networks that are available in the large towns, while satellite broadband connectivity through VSAT technology is common.

Wi-Fi is found in most lodges and hotels, though there may be a small fee to access it. Chcap prepaid SIM card Internet data bundles are available upon passport or work permit registration. Most large towns now have Internet cafés with secure PC terminals, access to all Web mail clients, and the usual photocopying, faxing, and printing services. It is always best to avoid financial transactions that may reveal passwords or personal details, and to delete your files and browsing history. Ask yourself: Has my anti-spyware been updated?

MAIL

The Zambia Postal Services Corporation (Zampost) reliably offers a range of services from routine mail collection and delivery (P.O. mailboxes are used) and the issuing of paper road tax discs to microfinance, such as the purchase of buses and reconditioned cars. For ordinary mail, Zampost works well for local and international destinations, and there is a registered mail service that allows for tracking, as well as a courier network. A number of companies provide parcel courier services, including DHL and FedEx.

CONCLUSION

For much of the world Zambia is relatively unknown. It is an African country that lacks the front-page coverage of drought, famine, wholesale corruption, and wars, and whose tourist industry doesn't have the brand recognition of Kenya and South Africa. Its beautiful landscape and untapped human and natural resources await discovery.

Zambia is a young country in a hurry to grow up, where the old, traditional way of life rubs shoulders with a global society in a twenty-first-century setting. Sleds and dugout canoes of the rural areas coexist with the electronic, high-tech world of urban life, and the shanty compounds share the African sky with country villages and luxurious mansions.

Perhaps the greatest challenge for Zambia is to find a way to resolve its enormous social inequalities and to take into account the needs of the majority. There is the feeling that, fine as the shopping malls, luxurious hotels, and game lodges are, there is a need to see that investment brings with it a commitment to benefit a greater number of people—development for all rather than a few—and the challenge is to make the economic and financial resources work for every Zambian.

The people of Zambia are its most important resource. Lively, fun loving, and always aspirational, the irrepressible Zambian character moves across a contradictory panorama. A country to invest in? Perhaps. A country to visit? Definitely!

Further Reading

Addison, Corban. *The Garden of Burning Sand.* New York: Quercus, 2014

Banda-Aaku, Ellen. *Patchwork.* Johannesburg: Penguin Books, 2011.

Fuller, Alexandra. *Cocktail Hour Under the Tree of Forgetfulness.* London: Simon & Schuster, 2011.

Fuller, Alexandra. *Leaving Before the Rains Come.* London: Harvill Secker, 2015.

Koloko, Leonard. *Zambian Music Legends.* USA: Lulu.com, 2012.

Lamb, Christina. *The Africa House: The True Story of an English Gentleman and his African Dream.* London: Viking, 1999.

Livingstone, David. *Narrative of an Expedition to the Zambesi and its Tributaries; and of the Discovery of the Lakes Shira and Nyassa, 1858–1864.* London: John Murray, 1865.

Loh, Adeline. *Peeing in the Bush.* Selangor, Malaysia, MPH Publishing, 2013.

Mwakikagile, Godfrey. *Zambia: Life in an African Country.* Dar es Salaam: New Africa Press, 2010.

Sandham, Fran. *Traversa.* London: Duckworth Overlook, 2007

Taylor, Scott D. *Culture and Customs of Zambia.* Westport, Connecticut: Greenwood Press, 2006.

culture smart! zambia

Index

accommodation 133–7
address, forms of 86–8
adultery 83, 89
Africa, Zambia and 48–9
African Union Peace and Security Council 49
age composition 10, 42
agriculture 45–7
AIDS 42, 74, 76, 77, 89, 92, 145, 148
air travel 124, 126, 127
annual leave 147–8
apartments 95, 96
area 8, 10
arts and crafts 121–2
Asian community 23
athletics 117
attitudes 50–63

Bangweulu, Lake/ Wetlands 8, 12, 123, 135–6
Bantu-speaking people 25–6
baptism 73–4
Barotse Floodplain 15, 16
basketware 121–2
beer 104–5, 113
Bemba people 20, 77
    cousinships 84–5
    history 26, 27, 29
    initiation ceremonies 71
    language 156–7
    marriage 82
bigamy 83
bilharzia 138
Blixen, Karen 12
body language 158
border crossings 124–6
boxing 116–17
breastfeeding 99
brewing 104–5
bribes 155
British Overseas Management Administration (BOMA) 19
British protectorate 32
British South African Company (BSAC) 31–2, 33
burial sites 52, 75–6
buses, intercity 128–9
bush protein 102–3

business briefing 140–55
business cards 148–9
business culture 143–4

casinos 115
cattle 80
celebrity, cult of 62
cell phones 161–2
censorship 159–60
Central African Plateau 12–13
character 9, 50–1
Chewa people 20, 27, 71, 72
chikanda (African polony) 101
children 42–3, 98–9
Chiluba, Frederick 56, 108
Chinese community 23, 24, 63
chitenge (traditional garment) 107–8, 122
Christianity 30, 31, 56–7
cinemas 114–15
circumcision 70
clay eating 73
climate 10, 17–18
clothing 92–3, 107–9
clubs and societies 86
colonial rule 32–5
coming of age ceremonies 70–1
Common Market for East and Central Africa (COMESA) 49
Commonwealth 35
communications 156–63
contracts 150
conversation 91–2
copper industry 10, 19, 32, 42, 43–4
corruption 151, 153–5
cousinships 84–5
crafts 121–2
cremations 76
cricket 117
currency 11
customs and traditions 64–83

daily life 97–9
dance 119–20

demonstrations of affection 51, 89
diplomacy, business 150
dress code
    business 148
    invitation events 92–3
drinks 104–5, 113
driving 130–2
Dutch Voortrekkers 27

early man 24–5
eating out 112–13
economy 36–7, 42–8
education 109–11
    for girls 55, 98
elections 38, 39
electricity 11, 44–5
emeralds 45
English language 63, 140, 156, 157
ethnic makeup 10, 18–24
European settlers 27–32
expatriates 86
    workers 146
extended family 42, 51, 53–4, 99
eye contact 158

family 51–4
fashion 108–9
Federation of Rhodesia and Nyasaland 34–5
ferries 125
festivals 67–9
fingers, eating with 93
fishing 47–8
food 99–103
    eating out 112–13
    invitation events 93
foreigners, attitudes toward 63
formal sector 62
fraud 151
friendships 84–93
funerals 74–6, 84

GDP 11, 42, 140
gender roles 54–5, 152
geography 10, 12–17
gift giving 152–3
golf 117
government 11, 39–40
Great Bangweulu Basin 17

greetings 87, 88–9

hair 106–7
hand-holding 51
handshakes 88–9, 149
Hatton, Denys Finch 12
healers 73
health 137–8
Hichilema, Hakainde
    38, 39
Hindus 23, 56
history 24–37
HIV 70, 74, 77, 138,
    145
home life 94–111
homosexuality,
    attitudes toward 59
hospitals 137
hotels 133–4
House of Chiefs 40
housing 94–7
humor 158
hunter-gatherers 25
huts 94–5

Ila people 22, 80, 84
immigration 125–6
independence 35
Indian community
    23, 63
informal sector 60–2
inheritance laws 78
initiation ceremonies
    70–1
insurance, health 137
International Monetary
    Fund 36, 37
international relations
    48–9
internet 11, 162–3
investment, foreign
    140, 141, 142–3,
    145–7
invitations 92–3

judicial system 40, 41,
    150–1

Kafue National Park 8,
    16, 134–5
Kafue River 13, 15
Kalahari sands 15
Kaonde people 22, 71
Kariba, Lake 8, 12,
    14–15, 122
Kasanka National Park
    31, 123, 136
Kaunda, Kenneth 19,
    33, 34, 35, 36–7,
    84, 108
Kewanika, Godwin 33

Kuomboka ceremony
    67–8, 123

labor 145–7
Lala people 22
land acquisition 142,
    150
languages 11, 87–8,
    156–8
legal considerations,
    business 150–1
leisure time 112–23
Lenje people 22
Lewanika, King 31, 68
Liemba (ferry) 125
life expectancy 11
literacy 11
Livingstone 32, 133
Livingstone, David 8,
    28, 29–31, 123
lobola (bride price) 51,
    55, 80–1, 82
lodges 133
Lower Zambezi
    National Park 134,
    135
Lozi people 15, 21–2,
    26, 28, 31, 67–8, 71,
    80, 84
Luangwa National Park
    122, 134
Luangwa River 13,
    15, 16
Lunda people 23, 26–7,
    32, 68–9
Lungu, Edgar 38
Lusaka 10, 33, 123, 133
Luvale people 69, 70, 71
Lykumbi Lyamizi
    ceremony 69

mail 163
Makishi masquerade
    69, 70
malaria 138
manufacturing 48,
    143, 144
markets 61, 122
marriage 55, 78–83
masks 121
meat 101, 103
media 11, 159–61
medicine, traditional
    71–3
meetings 148–9
Mfecane ("the
    crushing") 27–8
minibuses 129–30
missionaries 31
mixed-race
    relationships 90–1

money, lending 91
Movement for
    Multiparty
    Democracy (MMD)
    37
Multi-Facility
    Economic Zones
    (MFEZ) 142
music 114, 115, 118–20
Muslims 23, 56
Mweru, Lake 12

national parks 134
nationalism 33–5
natural resources 8, 10,
    43–5, 140
Nc'wala ceremony 67
negotiations 150
New Economic
    Recovery Program
    (NERP) 37
newspapers 159, 160
Ngoni people 20–1
    cousinships 84–5
    history 27, 28, 32
    Nc'wala ceremony
    67
NGOs 145
nightlife 114–15
Nkumbula, Harry 33
Northern Rhodesia
    32–5
Northern Rhodesia
    African National
    Congress 33
Northern Rhodesia
    Congress 33
Nsenga people 20
nshima (maize
    porridge) 99–100
nuclear power 45
Nyanja language 156–7

office hours 147
opposite sex 89–90
orphans 42, 74

Patriotic Front (PF)
    38, 39
payday 105
Pentecostal movement
    56–7, 74
people 18–24
personnel 145–8
politics 37–9, 49
polo 117–18
polygamy 72, 83
population 10, 24, 42–3
Portuguese 28–9
poverty 42, 96, 145
prehistory 24–5

presentations 149
press 159, 160
proverbs 66
provinces 18
public holidays 64–5

radio 11, 159, 161
rail travel 124, 125, 127–8
rainfall 17–18
religion 11, 56–9
Republic of Zambia 35
restaurants 112–13
Rhodes, Cecil 31, 32
road travel 124–5, 130–2

safety 139
Sata, Michael 38, 39, 84–5
schistosomiasis 138
schools 109–11
Scott, Guy 39
seasons 10
security 96
self-employment 144
sex, and the law 55
sexual cleaning 77–8
Shaka kaSenzangakhona 27, 28
shanty compounds 95–6
Shiwa Ngandu Estates 136–7
"side-chicks" 83
slave trade 28–9
soccer 115–16
socializing 85–6
sorcery 57–9
Southern African Development Community (SADC) 49
Southern Rhodesia 31, 33, 34
speeches 93
sports 115–18
state of emergency 34
Stone Age 24, 25

storytelling, traditional 65–6
street food 112
street vending 61–2
sugar daddies/ mommies 89

Tanganyika, Lake 12, 125
tax incentives 141
taxis 130
telephones 161–2
television 11, 159, 160–1
temperatures 17–18
tenders 151
theatre 115
theft 139
time, attitudes toward 60
time zone 11
tipping 113
Tonga people 21, 27, 77, 80, 84
    initiation ceremonies 70, 71
traditional beliefs 57–9
traditions 64–83
travel
    around towns 129–30
    arrival 124–6
    getting around 127–9
    roads and driving 130–2
tribal ceremonies, traditional 67–9
tribal relationships 84
Tumbuka people 20, 71

unemployment 42
United National Independence Party (UNIP) 19, 35, 36, 37
United Party for National Development (UPND) 38, 39
universities 62, 111

vaccinations 137–8
values 50–63
vegetarians and vegans 113
Victoria Falls 8, 10, 12, 14, 123, 126, 133–4
village life 94–5, 105–6
visas 125–6
vocabulary, new 157–8

wealth, and status 62–3
weddings 82–3, 84
Welensky, Roy 34
white community 23
WI-FI 163
wildlife 12, 123, 134–7
wine 113
witchcraft 57–9, 78
women
    in business 151–2
    child brides 55, 78–9
    female initiation 70–1, 79
    role of 54–5, 83, 97–8
    safety 90
    widows 77–8
work 60–2, 143–4
World Bank 36, 37, 140, 151, 153

yellow fever 137–8

Zambezi River 8, 12, 13–15, 67, 133–4, 138
Zambia African National Congress (ZANC) 34, 35
Zambia Association of Manufacturers (ZAM) 144
Zambia Chamber of Commerce and Industry (ZACCI) 144
Zambia Development Agency (ZDA) 142
Zimbabwe 31–2
Zulus 27–8

Acknowledgments

To Albina, my wife—a valuable, loving reference book, whose pages were always opened whenever I needed assistance. To the country of Zambia, which gave me opportunities and a passion for Africa.